D0946926

IRCC
ROOM
INDIAN
RIVER
COMMUNITY
COLLEGE
Chas.
Indian
ibrary
ce, Fla.

ASR-2223

Walker Percy's Feminine Characters

Walker Percy's Feminine Characters

edited by
Lewis A. Lawson and Elzbieta H. Oleksy

The Whitston Publishing Company
Troy, New York
1995

Library of Congress Catalog Card Number 94-62092

ISBN 0-87875-456-3

Printed in the United States of America

Contents

Introduction

In the extensive scholarship devoted to Walker Percy's six published novels, relatively little attention has been given to gender and even less to women characters. Undoubtedly this omission results from the fact that, with the exception of Allie Huger in *The Second Coming* (1980), the Percy protagonist is always a male. But the omission is not justified by that fact, for women—as mothers, daughters, wives, and lovers—figure abundantly in Percy's fiction, from his first published novel, the National Book Award winner *The Moviegoer* (1961), to his last, *The Thanatos Syndrome* (1987). Yet so far they have claimed very little critical attention. Michael Kobre, reviewing Jan Nordby Gretlund and Karl-Heinz Westarp's collection of papers *Walker Percy: Novelist and Philosopher* in 1992, laments the absence of discussion (with the single exception of Elzbieta H. Oleksy's paper on misogny in *Lancelot*) of what he considers "one of the most problematic aspects of Percy's fiction: his presentation of women characters."[1] The present collection aims at filling in this gap.

Percy wrote four novels before 1980. Besides *The Moviegoer* and *Lancelot*, there were *The Last Gentleman* (1966) and *Love in the Ruins* (1971). But as late as 1980 there had been only two brief references to the way women fare in Percy's fiction. In 1974 John F. Zeugner, writing about *Love in the Ruins*, says of Percy that "he has always been something of a male chauvinist" and that women in Percy's fiction are "remarkably two dimensional."[2] In the recently published interview with Percy, conducted by Dorothy H. Kitchings in 1979, Percy explains why his fictional women are such flat characters. He says: "I was brought up in a male tradition which is very commonplace in the South in which it is very hard to get the two together; to get the sexual woman together with a 'lady'."[3] The lady/whore dichotomy in Percy's fiction becomes the subject of more extensive discussion in two interviews conducted in the

Eighties, with Jan Nordby Gretlund (1981)[4] and with Jo Gulledge (1984),[5] and in Jac Tharpe's study of Percy (1983).[6] To Gretlund's accusation that women get "harsh treatment" from Percy and that there are no "normal" women in his fiction, Percy takes the blame, but then interestingly adds that he does not understand the phenomenon of a "normal" woman and says that he "can only understand [a woman] if she is as neurotic" as he is. On the same note, to Gulledge's accusation that women in his fiction are stereotyped into an "angelism/bestialism situation," Percy says that he is gender-democratic as regards bestialism in people but adds that "using a woman [is] a better way to bring out the demoniac spirit of sexuality." The idea, he further explains, came from the Phil Donahue show, where he heard a "woman analyst . . . who did a survey asking women their most commonly experienced dreams, sexual fantasies in their dreams. It was being assaulted." Gulledge rightly questions the reliability of the source, but the conversation (unfortunately) veers into other topics. Jac Tharpe's *Walker Percy* also concentrates on the lady/whore dichotomy, with the conclusion that Percy "shows no interest in the question of women's rights" (26-27). The early phase of critical regard for Percy's portrayal of women reached a climax in Houston, at the 1980 Modern Language Association Convention, most appropriately, when Cleanth Brooks, in treating Percy's "southernness," praised his "little bouquet of descriptions of Southern women":

> A novelist of manners will usually exhibit his powers to best advantage in this area, for it is traditionally the women who establish and maintain the current code of manners. On this subject of the Southern woman, Percy writes with both gusto and sensitive discrimination.[7]

By the mid-Eighties critical assessment of Percy's characterization of women began to attain a much higher level of complexity and reserve. Francine Du Plessix Gray may stand as representative of those who were less than charmed by him, for she wrote—in her review of *Lost in the Cosmos* (1983), not a fiction but a heated evaluation of a contemporary culture—that " . . . Mr. Percy's stand on women is hardly more palatable" than " . . . is a hostility toward homosexuals in his pages that is particularly odious."[8] Ironically, Percy's standing among many readers was declining even at the time when he was acknowledging the weakness of his earlier attempts at creating autonomous fictional women. He told Edmund Fuller of his satisfaction with the female protagonist in *The Second Coming*:

> I'm very happy about this girl, Allie. Women sometimes

> have charged me with not knowing anything about women, which may be true, but I like what I have done with Allie. I think she is my most successful woman character.[9]

There is considerable wariness toward even Allie, though. For she is not excluded in this generalization made by Donna Kelleher Darden: "It is the strength of the woman who lives with the Southern intellectual man described by Walter [sic] Percy, who must also be either crazy or alcoholic to survive."[10] Cool to Percy's earlier protagonists, John Edward Hardy sees both Will Barrett and "the third-person narrator of *The Second Coming*" as "male chauvinist" as Binx Bolling in *The Moviegoer* (190): "The man is in charge" (191),[11] so Allie must inevitably be inferior. In an excellent study of the theme of the religious quest in Percy's fiction, *Walker Percy: Books of Revelations*, Gary Ciuba argues convincingly:

> Although Percy's typically male seekers seem more open to discovering their life in God, the women they have loved are never clearly shown to have come as far in their wayfaring. Sometimes they are not even present at the close. When Allison Sutter disappears from the final pages of 'The Gramercy Winner' [an unpublished novel], she almost sets the pattern for Kitty, Anna, and Lucy to be absent at the conclusion of Percy's later apocalypses. Even when such women of faith as Kate, Ellen, and Allie are depicted as still living amid the ruins of these final scenes, they never achieve a religious understanding that receives the same affirmation in the novel as the spiritual vision of Binx, Tom, and Will. . . . Indeed, Percy's searchers usually find it more compatible to talk about the progress of their souls with other men . . .[12]

If Percy's women characters do not receive religious parity, according to Ciuba, neither, according to Elzbieta Oleksy, do they receive philosophic parity. In *Plight in Common: Hawthorne and Percy*,[13] she argues that, given Percy's existentialist beliefs, he was virtually unable to conceive a meaningful relationship between his male and female characters: concentrating on a single subjectivity, invariably male, Percy had to relegate his female characters to the position of "other." When this influence spent itself, Percy explored the possibility of an intersubjective communion, the full realization of which he achieved in *The Second Coming*. Percy's excellent biographer Jay Tolson uses life to account for the undeveloped aspects of Percy's fictional women that Ciuba and Oleksy discern: "both in his fiction and in his life" Percy had "a problem in seeing the person behind the ideal."[14]

Also approaching *The Second Coming* through its language

theme—and thereby elevating Allie as Percy's most successful female character—are two essays that preceded Oleksy: Michael Pearson, "Language and Love in Walker Percy's *The Second Coming*," *Southern Literary Journal*, 20 (Fall 1987), 89-100, and Colleen M. Tremonte, "The Poet-Prophet and Feminine Capability in Walker Percy's *The Second Coming*," *The Mississippi Quarterly*, 43 (Spring 1990), 173-181.

What the scholarship of the past few years has shown most clearly is that the problem of Percy's treatment of his fictional women cannot be dealt with as an isolated phenomenon, susceptible of a simple conclusion. The problem must, on the contrary, be viewed in light of earlier issues that have been raised in the criticism of his work, such as his "southernness" or his cultural conservatism, even as it must be aligned with newer forms of scrutiny, such as gender studies, various forms of psychological analysis, and language studies. Each of the essays to follow addresses itself to a significant aspect of this multifaceted problem.

Three essays deal with *The Moviegoer*, Percy's first published novel and probably best known, in part because of its existentialist context. In "The Dream Screen in *The Moviegoer*" Lewis Lawson proposes that the key image of "the moviegoer" alludes to Binx Bolling's fantasy of returning to the womb, maternal security, the loss of which accounts for his alienation. In "Gesture and Style in *The Moviegoer*" Emory Elliott argues that Binx Bolling, in the tradition of the American literary protagonist, is on a metaphysical quest, but that Kate Cutrer has the gumption to position herself as his goal. In "The Exclusionary Nature of *The Moviegoer*" Timothy K. Nixon argues that the nature of the novel is so "male-centered" that a woman reader who identifies with Binx Bolling would experience herself as "the other."

Four essays deal with the character of Will Barrett. In "Keeping Quentin Compson Alive: *The Last Gentleman, The Second Coming*, and the Problem of Masculinity" Susan Donaldson deftly contrasts Percy's Will Barrett with Faulkner's Quentin Compson, to argue that while Will learns to bear it well it enough to reject suicide, he never learns to reject the habitude that found honor in suicide. In "'The Cave . . . the Fence': A Lacanian Reading of Walker Percy's *The Second Coming*" Doreen Fowler argues that "Will, who has renounced death, finds death no matter which way he turns. If he chooses Father Weatherbee, he creates the self through a violent rupturing, a form of castration and death; if he chooses Allison, he reintegrates with his absent center and is reabsorbed into the universe, another form of castration and death." In "The Privilege of Maternity: Teaching Language and Love in *The Second Coming*" Shelley Jackson, stimulated by Carol Gilligan and Nancy Chodorow, shows how Allie Huger, acting as mother-nurturer, enables Will Barrett to achieve a trust in love and a trust in language as a medium for love. Elinor Ann Walker's "Rereading Allison Huger: Making Silence Signify in *The Second Coming*" pairs nicely with Shelly Jackson's essay, for it traces the development of Allie's belief in her own voice, a confidence that she would have to have before she could nurture Will.

Two general essays conclude the collection. In "A Gentleness with Women: Loving, Caring, and Sexual Dilemmas in Walker Percy's Fiction," Anneke Leenhouts treats more broadly and more extensively the Southern honor code that Susan Donaldson sees afflicting Quentin Compson and Will Barrett: she concludes that masculine domination is not yet gone with the wind. And, appropriately, Elzbieta H. Oleksy, in "From Silence and Madness to the Exchange That Multiplies: Walker Percy and the Woman Question," uses her ultimate position to summarize and strengthen all that has gone before. Using Kierkegaard as a representative of the modern tradition of the isolated subjectivity and Marcel as a representative of the ancient but too often forgotten tradition of intersubjectivity, she traces Percy's wayfaring from *The Moviegoer*, with its spectatorial consciousness of the other, to *The Second Coming*, with its subjects serving as mirrors for each other.

Elzbieta H. Oleksy and Lewis A. Lawson

Works Cited

[1] "Apocalyptics and Existentialism: Percy Criticism at a Crossroad," *Mississippi Quarterly* 46 (Winter 1992-93): 134.

[2] "Walker Percy and Gabriel Marcel: The Castaway and the Wayfarer," *Mississippi Quarterly* 28 (Winter 1984): 44.

[3] "An Interview with Walker Percy," in *More Conversations with Walker Percy*, eds. Lewis A. Lawson and Victor A. Kramer (Jackson: University Press of Mississippi, 1993) 9.

[4] "Laying the Ghost of Marcus Aurelius?", in *Conversations with Walker Percy*, eds. Lewis A. Lawson and Victor A. Kramer (Jackson: University Press of Mississippi, 1985) 212.

[5] "The Reentry Option," in *Conversations with Walker Percy* 288.

[6] *Walker Percy* (Boston: Twayne Publishers, 1983).

[7] "The Southernness of Walker Percy," *South Carolina Review* 13 (Spring 1981): 35.

[8] "A Pop-Socratic Survey of Despair," *New York Times Book Review* June 5, 1983: 9.

[9] "A Conversation with Novelist Walker Percy," *Conversations with Walker Percy* 188.

[10] "Southern Women Writing about Southern Women: Jill McCorkle, Lisa Alther, Gail Godwin, Ellen Gilchrist, and Lee Smith," in *Southern Women*, ed. Caroline Matheny Dillman (New York: Hemisphere, 1988).

[11] *The Fiction of Walker Percy* (Urbana: University of Illinois Press, 1987).

[12] (Athens: University of Georgia Press, 1991) 21.

[13] (New York: Peter Lang, 1993).

[14] *Pilgrim in the Ruins: A Life of Walker Percy* (New York: Simon and Schuster, 1992) 93.

The Dream Screen in *The Moviegoer*

Lewis A. Lawson

It is not often noted, but the narrative proper of Walker Percy's *The Moviegoer* (1961), while it offers a very seductive "virtual present," is actually a re-presenting of selected events from an eight-day period that occurred at some point over a year in the past.[1] The Epilogue establishes the fact that Binx has been representing to himself the feelings that he had earlier experienced, but had not been able to articulate; Percy's technique is illuminated by Charles Sanders Peirce's model of consciousness: the self-which-is silently converses with the self-which-is-just-coming-to-be. Percy implies such a strategy in "From Facts to Fiction":

> When I sat down to write *The Moviegoer*, I was very much aware of discarding the conventional notions of a plot and a set of characters, discarded because the traditional concept of plot-and-character itself reflects a view of reality which has been called into question. Rather would I begin with a *man* who finds himself in a *world*, a very concrete man who is located in a very concrete place and time. Such a man might be represented as *coming to himself* . . . (9)

The man coming to himself is the Binx who has selected and arranged a group of images so that their form conveys, represents, names his feelings to himself. These images—and, indeed, the form they take—would have been formed from and influenced by dreams, so that it is appropriate that dreams and dreaming are inescapably prominent in the content of the narrative. The boy Binx

---

This essay was previously published in *Papers on Language and Literature*, 30 (Winter 1994), 25-56, and is reprinted here by generous permission of Brian Abel Ragen, co-editor, *PLL*.

who got "excited" about Freud's *Interpretation of Dreams* (138), but was rebuffed by his mother's lack of interest, the thirty-year old Binx who is unconsciously driven by dreams caused by the rebuffing mother to "act out," and is in the Epilogue the Binx who, by virtue of his conversion to Christianity (a restitution of the lost object), can now understand and name his past condition for himself.

During the eight days of his life that he recollects, Binx goes to the movies four times and refers to twelve identified and several unidentified movies. There is some truth to the diagnosis of Binx provided by Harvey R. Greenberg:

> One encounters chronic moviemania in rigid, inhibited types who feel exquisitely uncomfortable when forced into close interpersonal contact. Safe only in well-defined social situations, intolerably anxious if called upon to improvise, these people sleepwalk through the day's routine and only come alive at second hand, as proxy participants in the adventures of their screen idols. (Walker Percy's elegant novel *The Moviegoer* describes such a case.) (4)

But there is not enough to Greenberg's analysis. Binx shows no interest in cinematographic technique, nor indeed does he say much about acting technique; he comments on a film narrative or a character's action only if it re-presents in some way some aspect of his life. The movie screen is his dream screen, in the sense that Robert T. Eberwein describes the connection between the two screens in *Film and the Dream Screen*.

Throughout Binx's recollection it is the image of the movie theater, rather than the memory of a specific movie, which offers the more evocative impression. Esther Harding interprets a theater as a dream symbol: "This is the place where the typical stories of a man's life are shown, that is, the mythogems are presented to consciousness" (171). When Binx describes his "neighborhood theater in Gentilly" (7)—the evocative *gen* the source of so many birth-related words—he emphasizes its form, not its function of presenting constantly changing attractions: the theater "has permanent lettering on the front of the marquee reading: Where Happiness Costs So Little" (7). He adds, "[t]he fact is I am quite happy in a movie, even a bad movie," his choice of preposition suggesting the primacy of the experience of enclosure in his moviegoing. It is not too much to suggest that he experiences "*nyctophilia*," defined by Bertram Lewin as "an erotic pleasure in darkness, which enters as a wish-fulfillment element in fantasies of being in the 'womb,' or more properly, as the German word *Mutterleib* suggests, of being in the mother's body" (*The Image* 40). In short, Binx has a need, whether by dreaming or by moviegoing, to regress to "the first incestuous objects of the libido," as Freud puts it (350).

When Binx begins his recollection, he indicates that he had been awakened to the possibility of a search by a dream of his wounding in the Korean War, an event to which he will refer several times in his narrative. That event was no doubt traumatic, yet the imagery which Binx uses to describe it suggests that that memory "screens" a memory of a more primal wounding:

> I remembered the first time the search occurred to me. I came to myself under a chindolea bush. . . . My shoulder didn't hurt but it was pressed hard against the ground as if somebody sat on me. (10-11)
>
> Only once in my life was the grip of everydayness broken: when I lay bleeding in a ditch. (145)

The first citation is made meaningful by J. C. Flugel's comment about anxiety, during his discussion of "birth fantasies." Tracing the word *anxiety* back to the Sanskrit *anhus*, meaning "narrowness or constriction," he argues that anxiety "bears witness to the fundamental association of fear with pressure and shortness of breath, which—the former owing to the passage through the narrow vagina, the latter to the interruption of the foetal circulation—constitute the most menacing and terrifying aspects of the birth process" (70). The second citation is a rather vivid description of the moment of birth.

If Binx's memory of his war wound is a re-presentation of his birth trauma, it is significantly appropriate that he thinks of the wound in connection with all three women who play psycho-sexual roles in his life. As a result of the car collision on their way to the Gulf Coast, Sharon has to cut away Binx's T-shirt:

> I was shot through the shoulder—a decent wound, as decent as any ever inflicted on Rory Calhoun or Tony Curtis. After all it could have been in the buttocks or genitals—or nose. Decent except that the fragment nicked the apex of my pleura and got me a collapsed lung and a big roaring empyema. (126)

It is noteworthy that Binx's wounding results in a lung condition, for there is a long tradition of suspecting nostalgia as a cause of some lung conditions (Rosen 448-50). When Sharon, the mother substitute, sees the scar, she obligingly becomes maternal: "Come on now, son, where did you get that?" (126). Binx is jubilant, must think that his seduction is as good as done. Later, at the fishing camp, Binx uses the episode of his wounding to try to get his mother to understand how he has felt about his entire life: "What I am trying to tell you is that nothing seemed worth doing except something I couldn't even remember" (158). In other words, through the screening process he represses any recognition of the primal wound and therefore regresses in fantasy and in acted-out Don Juan behavior. And, finally, when he realizes in Chicago that he is falling in love with Kate, he says: "There I see her plain, see plain for the first time since I lay wounded in a ditch and watched an Oriental finch scratching around in the leaves . . ." (206). Binx implies that his mental visualization is finally free of "the parent in the percept."[2] His ability to choose an appropriate mate enables him to transcend his yearning for the mother who will not nurture.

The first movie that Binx mentions is not one that he actually attends during the time being recollected; this strategy gives Binx the opportunity to imply from the outset that his moviegoing is *a la recherche du temps perdu*—almost all of the movies to which he refers are re-releases. Since it is unidentified by title—thus losing its individuality, becoming a generic movie—the movie he mentions is just one that he "saw last month out by Lake Pontchartrain" (4) with his then-sweetheart Linda. What he says about the theater, little as it is, says much about his psychosexual regression: "[a] strong wind whipped the waves against the seawall; even inside you could hear the racket" (4), and "the theater was almost empty, which was pleasant for me" (5). For Binx the theater replicates his intrauterine residence, which he would of course like not to share.

In this regard, it is significant that the theater is "out by Lake Pontchartrain" and Binx has a date with him. Binx is acting out Sandor Ferenczi's contention that man has a drive to water as it symbolizes his phylogenetic history both as a fish and as a foetus. Such a drive activates the fantasy of copulating with the mother; since this activity is forbidden, the actual copulation must occur with a substitute object, which is what Binx's succession of secretaries represents, all of whom he takes to the Gulf Coast. Ferenczi's "situation of the penis in the vagina, the foetus in the uterus, and the fish in the water" (45) will surface again.

In his state of regression from the reality-principle, as Freud called it, Binx would have watched this movie closely:

> The movie was about a man who lost his memory in an accident and as a result lost everything: his family, his friends, his money. He found himself a stranger in a strange city. Here he had to make a fresh start, find a new place to live, a new job, a new girl. It was supposed to be a tragedy, his losing all this, and he seemed to suf-

> fer a great deal. On the other hand things were not so bad after all. In no time he found a very picturesque place to live, a houseboat on the river, and a very handsome girl, the local librarian. (4-5)

The Thalassan content of the movie thus replicates the meaning that the theater has for Binx.

The theme of the movie is "[a]mnesia[,] . . . the perfect device of rotation."[3] Binx very carefully neglects the ending, stopping his recapitulation at the point of rotational triumph, at which point the ego-hero has reached Eden, "a very picturesque houseboat on the river," and an ideal mother-substitute, "the local librarian." For if rotation climaxes, post-coital depression is inevitable; rotation's "only term is suicide or self loss" (Percy, "The Man" 95). Just a few minutes later, Binx admits premature withdrawal from the plot:

> The movies are onto the search, but they screw it up. The search always ends in despair. They like to show a fellow coming to himself in a strange place—but what does he do? He takes up with the local librarian, sets up about proving to the local children what a nice fellow he is, and settles down with a vengeance. In two weeks time he is so sunk in everydayness that he might just as well be dead. (13)

Binx has already admitted that his rotation with Linda is over.

There is one final comment to be made about this first description of moviegoing. Binx always places himself in a movie theater, his fantasy substitute for the maternal womb, when he illustrates, either by implication or by explication, the various aspects of his theory of psychology (certification, alienation, rotation, and aesthetic repetition). He very clearly situates his intellect within a matrix of mother-loss.

Thus, early on Wednesday morning, before Binx ventures into his objective-empirical world (as a young bachelor stockbroker in New Orleans, scion of a very old Louisiana family), he has already—by using Mrs. Langer's analogy, "[c]inema is 'like' dream"—described his *felt life*. For all the apparent specificity and solidity of Binx's world, Gentilly is "very spacious and airy and seems to stretch out like a field under the sky" (9-10); if such a description does not convey enough *unheimlichkeit*, then Binx's response to the homes near the lake should be noted: "at this hour of dawn they are forlorn. A sadness settles over them like a fog from the lake" (84). This white mist—to be exposed before the week is out, at Binx's mother's fishing camp—is now just "a fog of uneasiness, a thin gas of malaise" (18):

> What is the malaise? you ask. The malaise is the pain of

> loss. The world is lost to you, the world and people in it, and there remains only you and the world and you no more able to be in the world than Banquo's ghost. (120)

On Wednesday night, Binx goes go to a movie, *Panic in the Streets*, with his Aunt Emily's stepdaughter Kate. In the movie Richard Widmark plays a public health inspector who discovers "that a culture of cholera bacilli has gotten loose in the city. . . . There is a scene which shows the very neighborhood of the theater" (63). Such a movie, focusing upon the objective-empirical world, emphasizes the values of its worldview. Thus, for people indoctrinated with that worldview, to see the familiar re-presented by a visual apparatus is to see heightened reality. Such a movie would seem to hold no promise for Binx, but there is that phenomenon of—to borrow the language of "The Man on the Train"—"the triumphant reversal of alienation through its representing" (93). Binx calls this "phenomenon of moviegoing . . . certification" (63):

> Nowadays when a person lives somewhere, in a neighborhood, the place is not certified for him. More than likely he will live there sadly and the emptiness which is inside him will expand until it evacuates the entire neighborhood. But if he sees a movie which shows his very neighborhood, it becomes possible for him to live, for a time at least, as a person who is Somewhere and not Anywhere. (63)

As a curative for emptiness—malaise, "the pain of loss"—such a reversal is, however, a Band-Aid. Alienation endures.

And since it does, Binx must look for a rotatory deliverance: on Thursday morning he embarks upon the seduction of his new secretary, Sharon. Already he has begun to fantasize her as Aphrodite, seeing her as a golden creature (95).[4] Binx admits: "[d]esire for her is like a sorrow in my heart" (68). His description of his desire is no more exaggerated than is to be expected of a healthy twenty-nine year old man in the Big Easy, but the psychosexual ramifications of his desire are better appreciated with the aid of Robert Romanyshyn's phenomenology of desire, too long to be repeated here, except for its summary:

> If desire is the story of a homecoming, then it is the story of a home which is present *before* one's *consideration* of the heavens but paradoxically also absent until *after* this *consideration*. It is a home which does not exist but paradoxically always is, this home of desire. It is the home out of which dreams of paradise and tales of the gardens of Eden are born. It is the home we have never had but have always lived. (51-2)

Sharon, then, is the latest object to excite Binx's fantasy of the mother-land. As he secretively reads *Arabia Deserta* (68), a title which describes his life in Gentilly, he dreams of Sharon, the oasis, the place where the water is.

Charles M. Doughty's long trek to Mecca—as a disguised Christian among the Muslims—reminds Binx of how he came to undertake his "horizontal search." He had pursued a "vertical search"—an intellectual quest founded on Plato, currently manifested by objective-empiricism[5]—until he discovered that it left him "left over" (70), his adaptation of Sartre's *de trop*, the individual who is superfluous in any scientistic worldview. It happened in a hotel in Birmingham (the same city in which Walker Percy discovered alienation); Binx read *The Chemistry of Life*, which explained everything but himself, which is not chemical; he closed the book to go see *It Happened One Night*, which is offered, in "The Man on the Train," as an illustration of this movement: "Zone crossing is of such great moment to the alienated I because the latter is thereby able to explore the It while at the same time retaining his option of noncommitment" (88). Then, therefore, Binx adopted the "horizontal search," the alienated way, with its specious deliverances of short-term reversal, rotation, and aesthetic repetition. Disguised as successfully as Charles Doughty, Binx displays his noncommitment most apparently as he explores the *en soi* of his succession of secretaries.

On his way home on Thursday afternoon, Binx stops off at the Tivoli Theater. Since the theater as a form is the locus of Binx's womb fantasy, which often reveals itself in his hankering after such Eden-like places as oases and parks, the Tivoli, named after the famous Italian gardens, would have special appeal for him. The manager practically forces Binx to take a "sample look" (73) at a Jane Powell musical, but the cheerful outgoingness of the actress is enough to drive him to despair.

Yet one happy movie does not an alien make. Binx has to admit, "it was here in the Tivoli that I first discovered place and time, tasted it like okra" (75), during a re-release of *Red River* a couple of years before. It is Binx's recollection of the experience as a gustatory event which demands close attention; in *Film and the Dream Screen* Robert Eberwein bases the following paragraph on the thought of Julia Kristeva:

> The infant's relationship to its mother after birth can be described as a kind of 'semiotic' *chora*. . . . In its vocalizations and cries (these actions themselves revivals of more primitive activities engaged in within the womb), the infant tries to survive by calling for food. The

> mother responds to these anaclises by offering herself. Notice the similarity of the terms used by Kristeva to describe the mother and the kind of language one might use to describe the viewing situation in a theater. The mother sustains the infant by 'providing . . . an axis, a projection screen, a limit, a support for the infant's invocation . . .' The union of infant and mother in the semiotic *chora* fixes a 'space': orality, audition, vision: archaic modalities upon which the most precocious discretion emerges. The breast given and withdrawn; lamp light capturing the gaze; the intermittent sound of voices or music—these greet anaclisis, . . . hold it, and thus inhibit and absorb it in such a way that it is discharged and calmed through them. . . . Therefore, the breast, light, sound become a *there*; place, point, marker. . . . The mark of an archaic point, the initiation into 'space,' the 'chora.' . . . There is not yet an outside. (32)

In the Tivoli Binx had, to say it another way, become energized by a dream of repetition, by a desire to go back to the time of symbiosis, before breast was lost as language was gained. Thus he became the moviegoer.

Binx's recollection of the Tivoli experience reminds him of another movie:

> Once as I was travelling through the Midwest ten years ago I had a layover of three hours in Cincinnati. There was time to go see Joseph Cotten in *Holiday* at a neighborhood theater called the Altamont—but not before I had struck up an acquaintance with the ticket seller, a lady named Mrs. Clara James, and learned that she had seven grandchildren all living in Cincinnati. (75)

Binx mentions the ticket seller because he had just previously explained his dependence upon mediation:

> If I did not talk to the theater owner or the ticket seller, I should be lost, cut loose metaphysically speaking. I should be seeing one copy of a film which might be shown anywhere and at any time. It is possible to become a ghost and not know whether one is in a downtown Loews in Denver or suburban Bijou in Jacksonville.

The film experience, he realizes, could be a metaphor for the objective-empirical method: Cartesian reality is universal and eternal, with the human being reduced to being a spectator. But now that he is alienated from the objective-empirical, Binx knows that salvation—if there is to be any—will be local and immediate, spoken to his person by another person.

The Cincinnati movie occurs to Binx for several reasons having to do with a sense of place. For one thing, Cincinnati is the home of the famous Eden Park. The theater's name, Altamont, would remind him of the hometown of Thomas Wolfe (celebrated in "The Man on the Train" [95] as a practitioner of the repetitional movement in literature). Clara James might suggest Laura James, the mother-substitute for Eugene Gant in *Look Homeward, Angel*. The movie title, *Holiday*, suggests that Binx, in recalling the Tivoli, has been tempted to yearn for the *Urkinohaus*, the *Mutterleib*. The setting of the movie has an idyllic, Thalassan name, Lake Placid, especially in contrast to Saranac Lake, five miles down the road, where Walker Percy had to deal with both tuberculosis and alienation. The movie thematizes the contrast between objective-empirical values, contained in the marble-walled Seaton mansion, and object-relation values, contained in the playroom. Johnny Case arrives to become engaged to Julia Seaton, but when he meets her sister Linda, they fall in love. According to Timothy W. Johnson, the playroom "is Linda's refuge—a warm, intimate room filled with dreams, childhood mementos, . . . and a portrait of their [dead] mother over the fireplace" (759). The only trouble with Binx's recollection? The lead male actor was Cary Grant, not Joseph Cotten; like Binx's memory, all aesthetic repetitions are unreliable.

Escaping from Jane Powell, Binx reaches his apartment in the basement of the house of Mrs. Schexnaydre (pronounced locally "SCHEX nay der," but Gallo-psychoanalytically as "*chez* NAY dir"). However her name is pronounced, she is the "bad mother" for the ego-hero; Mrs. Schexnaydre's house is built on this mythological substrate:

> When [the hero] arrives at the nadir of mythological round, he undergoes a supreme ordeal and gains his reward. The triumph may be represented as the hero's sexual union with the goddess-mother of the world (sacred marriage), his recognition by the father-creator (father atonement), his own divinization (apotheosis) . . .: intrinsically it is an expansion of consciousness and therewith of being (illumination, transfiguration, freedom). The final work is that of the return. . . . (Campbell 246)

Mrs. Schexnaydre has three dogs—a fractionate Cerberus—but Binx most despises the one that he has nicknamed "Rosebud," in honor of its "large convoluted anus" (77). As a student of moviegoing, Binx must know that *Citizen Kane* hinges on an object named Rosebud, which is the key to understanding that Charles Foster Kane's destiny was determined by the loss of his mother (Mayne 116-9). Once Binx can get past "Rosebud," he can get to his bed, over which "hang two Currier and Ives prints of ice-skaters in

Central Park. How sad the little figures seem, skimming along in step! How sad the city seems!" (78) Early on Wednesday Binx had said: "I . . . once met a girl in Central Park, but it is not much to remember" (7). Thus he implies that while he can try to repress his thoughts during the day he cannot control the dreams that hang over his bed at night. With his mind still very much in the mood awakened by his memory of *Holiday*, he goes to a movie on Thursday night.

Nor should the type of movie he selects come as a surprise:

> Tonight, Thursday night, I carry out a successful experiment in repetition.
>
> Fourteen years ago, when I was a sophomore, I saw a western at the moviehouse on Freret Street, a place frequented by students and known to them as the Armpit. The movie was *The Oxbow Incident* and it was quite good. . . . Yesterday evening I noticed in the *Picayune* that another western was playing in the same theater. (79)

When he and Kate come out of the movie, Binx says, "A successful repetition":

> What is a repetition? A repetition is the reenactment of past experience toward the end of isolating the time segment which has lapsed in order that it, the lapsed time, can be savored of itself and without the usual adulteration of events that clog time like peanuts in brittle. (79-80)

Binx's analogy between aesthetic repetition and peanut brittle (*sans* goobers) is like Ethel Spector Person's analogy between aesthetic repetition and the "lover's reel" in stressing that memory is selective (128). But Binx's analogy is additionally appropriate in stressing that experience, in his case, is gustatory:

> How, then, tasted my own fourteen years since *The Oxbow Incident*? As usual it eluded me. (80)

Binx's frustration is predicted by "The Man on the Train":

> Unlike rotation, [repetition] is of two kinds, the aesthetic and the existential, which literature accordingly polarizes. The aesthetic repetition captures the savor of repetition without surrendering the self as a locus of experience and possibility. When Proust tastes the piece of cake or Captain Ryder finds himself at Brideshead, the incident may serve as an occasion for either kind: an excursion into the interesting, a savoring of the past as experience, or two, the passionate quest in which the incident serves as a thread in the labyrinth to be followed at any cost. This latter, however, no matter how serious, cannot fail to be polarized by art, transmitting as the interesting. The question what does it mean to stand be-

> fore the house of one's childhood? is thus received in two different ways—one as an occasion for connoisseur sampling of a rare emotion, the other literally and seriously: what does it really mean? (95-6)

Since Binx is still engaged in rotation and aesthetic repetition, he has not surrendered "the self as a locus of experience and possibility" in order to pursue "the passionate quest." Thus he can only "savor" the past—Percy is consistent from genre to genre in attributing gustation to aesthetic repetition. But only in the novel, in that genre's covert way, will he ever admit that the gustatory response is ultimately *lactophilia*.

As if to demonstrate his refusal to surrender to the passionate quest, Binx dedicates Friday and Saturday to the great rotation of seducing Sharon. He is so engrossed in his plan that he does not need to go to a movie on Friday night, just watches a little television. Then, by noon on Saturday, he has persuaded Sharon to go to the beach with him. Once in his MG, she seems to intuit her role as a mother-substitute, for she begins to address him as "son" (124) or "boy" (132). Through a fortunate accident, Binx is able to impersonate "Rory Calhoun or Tony Curtis" (126), even "Bill Holden" (127), as one of them would appear if he was playing a wounded war hero; Sharon is so captivated and maternal that Binx has milk on his mind as they take the ferry out to Ship Island. He is surrounded by "milk white" (219) country children while the boat is "chuffing through the thin milky waters of Mississippi Sound" (129).[6]

Binx perfectly captures the excitement when one returns to the beach:

> Over the hillock lies the open sea. The difference is very great: first, this sleazy backwater, then the great blue ocean. The beach is clean and a big surf is rolling in; the water in the middle distance is green and lathered. You come over the hillock and your heart lifts up; your old sad music comes into the major. (130)

But Binx's especial excitement is suggested by a comment made by D. W. Winnicott about a line by Tagore, "On the seashore of endless worlds, children play":

> In my adolescence I had no idea what it could mean but it found a place in me, and its imprint has not yet faded.
>
> When I first became a Freudian I *knew* what it meant. The sea and the shore represented endless intercourse between man and woman, and the child emerged from this union to have a brief moment before becoming in turn adult or parent. Then, as a student of unconscious symbolism, I *knew* (one always *knows*) that the sea is the

> mother, and onto the seashore the child is born. Babies come up out of the sea and are spewed out upon the land, like Jonah from the whale. So now the seashore was the mother's body, after a child is born and the mother and now viable baby are getting to know each other. (Muensterberger 5-6)

With such an emotional investment, Binx easily fantasizes Sharon as Aphrodite, born of the white foam:

> She wades out ahead of me, turning to and fro, hands outstretched to the water and sweeping it before her. Now and then she raises her hands to her head as if she were placing a crown and combs back her hair with the last two fingers. The green water foams . . . (130)

As Aphrodite—"originally a mother goddess," according to Michael Balint (93)—Sharon plays her role to perfection: "Come on, son. I'm going to give you some beer" (131). With his gustatory need met, no wonder that Binx can hardly wait for the next movement: "Once when she gets up, I come up on my knees and embrace her golden thighs, such a fine strapping armful they are" (132). Then he pays her full homage: "'Sweetheart, I'll never turn you loose.' Mother of all living, what an armful" (132). According to some etymologies, "mother of the living" is the meaning of the name *Eve*, so that Binx must be convinced that he is pretty close to Paradise. By the time the moon rises, Sharon has agreed to visit Binx's mother's fishing camp (136). While he has already admitted that Sharon, as a rotation object, is not so magnetic as she was, even so the pull of his mother's fishing camp as a locus of aesthetic repetition is so great that he still means to seduce her there, to fulfill Ferenczi's "situation of the penis in the vagina, the foetus in the uterus, and the fish in the water." He will return to the womb *on* his mother's place, if not *in* her place.

But his mother is at the camp, surrounded by the six surviving children of her second marriage. With justification, Binx thinks of the *Titanic*, another doomed maiden voyage. For the moviegoer, this will not be *A Night to Remember*. Just moments before, Sharon had given him the penultimate promise: "She had become tender toward me and now and then presses my cheek with her hand" (136). Such caresses activate the infant's reflex to suck (Brazelton and Cramer 51-2). The welcome that Binx receives from his mother is of a different order:

> 'Well, well, look who's here,' she says but does not look.
>
> Her hands dry, she rubs her nose vigorously with her three middle fingers held straight up. She has hay

> fever and crabs make it worse. It is a sound too well known to me to be remembered, this quick jiggle up and down and the little wet wringing noises under her fingers.
>
> We give each other a kiss or rather we press our cheeks together, Mother embracing my head with her wrist as if her hands were still wet. (137)

In effect receiving a brush-off from his mother, Binx ponders their relationship: "Sometimes I feel a son's love for her, or something like this, and try to give her a special greeting, but at this time she avoids my eye and gives me her cheek . . ." (137-8). When, after a while, he tries again to talk to her, he gets the impression that she is "as old and sly as Eve herself" (142), but this is not the bountiful Eve he had earlier imagined Sharon to be, but the Great Mother, whose preeminence was destroyed by the Yahwist author of Genesis. That goddess was often accompanied by a son-lover who was sacrificed to die, in order to perpetuate her power.

Understandably, Binx jumps at the opportunity to take his half-siblings and Sharon to the Moonlite Drive-In (143-4). There he can patter about rotations and aesthetic repetitions, as if his life were nothing but moviegoing. But later the real moviegoing begins:

> Three o'clock and suddenly awake amid the smell of dreams and of the years come back and peopled and blown away again like smoke. A young man am I, twenty nine, but I am as full of dreams as an ancient. At night the years come back and perch around my bed like ghosts. (144)

Here dreams have the attribute of smell—appropriately, since the sense of smell, like the sense of taste, is first directed to the mother's breast (Brazelton and Cramer, 60-1), which is the place on which dreams originate. Binx had broached the subject of his dreaming with a similar image:

> I dreamed of the war, no, not quite dreamed but woke with the taste of it in my mouth, the queasy-quince taste of 1951 and the Orient. (10)

Since the wartime experience is a screen memory for his infantile trauma, it should be accompanied by a taste.

As would be expected, Binx's previous extended discussion of his disturbed sleep occurs when he speaks of *chez Naydre*:

> . . . sometimes before dawn I awake with a violent start and for the rest of the night lie dozing yet wakeful and watchful. I have not slept soundly for many years. Not since the war when I was knocked out for two days have I really lost consciousness as a child loses consciousness

> in sleep and wakes to a new world not even remembering when he went to bed. I always know where I am and what time it is. Whenever I feel myself sinking toward a deep sleep, something always recalls me: 'Not so fast now. Suppose you should go to sleep and it should happen. What then?' Clearly nothing. Yet there I lie, wakeful and watchful and a sentinel, ears tuned to the slightest noise. I can even hear old Rosebud turning round and round in the azalea bushes before settling down. (83-4)

The simple explanation will not, however, suffice. The basement apartment, "as impersonal as motel room" (78), is a placeless place. Binx lives as a exile from Central Park, hounded by Rosebud, the witch's watchdog. Anyone caught in that situation would be tempted to regress, but fear that such regression might lead to extinction.

On the occasion in question, Binx had gotten up to walk to the lake. On his way he thought of another poor sleeper: "My father used to suffer from insomnia" (85). Binx's Aunt Emily has a memory of Binx's father as a "student prince" (50), taking "off helter-skelter up the Rhine . . . with a bottle of *Leibfraumilch* under one arm and *Wilhelm Meister* under the other." But apparently he never learned to wander from *Wilhelm,* nor did he find a sufficient supply of *Liebfraumilch,* even though he married a nurse. As Binx walks, he thinks of his mother's inability to respond to her husband's insomnia:

> Just at this hour of dawn I would be awakened by a terrible sound; my father crashing through the screen door, sleeping bag under his arm, his eyes crisscrossed by fatigue and by the sadness of these glimmering dawns. My mother, without meaning to, put a quietus on his hopes of sleep even more effectively than this forlorn hour. She had a way of summing up his doings in a phrase that took the heart out of him. He dreamed, I know, of a place of quiet breathing and a deep sleep under the stars and next to the sweet earth. She agreed. 'Honey, I'm all for it. I think we ought to get back to nature and I'd be right with you, Honey, if it wasn't for the chiggers. I'm chigger bait.' (85)

Binx's father continued his decline until he had no appetite at all. Then Binx's mother did mother her husband:

> I got his book. I remember it—it was a book called *The Greene Murder Case*. Everybody in the family read it. I began to read and he began to listen, and while I read, I fed him. (152-3)

But any reader of "The Man on the Train" knows that the effect of such a treatment is only temporary: "An Erle Stanley Gardner novel is a true exercise in alienation. A man who finishes his twentieth Perry Mason is that much nearer total despair than when he started" (83). Only the onset of World War II could rouse Binx's father from his torpor. Then—and this completes Binx's train of thought about his father—as a volunteer, Binx's father had died "in the wine dark sea" (25) off Crete. That his father had regressed to extinction is implied in Binx's bitter comment:

> He found a way to do both: to please [the family] and please himself. To leave. To do what he wanted to do and save old England doing it. And perhaps even carry off the grandest coup of all: to die. To win the big prize for them and for himself (but not even he dreamed he would succeed not only in dying but in dying in Crete in the wine dark sea). (157)

That he knows the source of his father's alienation Binx implies by his assertion that his father died with a copy of *A Shropshire Lad* in his pocket, mother-haunted A. E. Housman's great celebration of his nostalgia.[7]

When, then, Binx suddenly wakes at the fishing camp, he seems to experience nausea:

> . . . my old place is used up (places get used up by rotatory and repetitive use) and when I awake, I awake in the grip of everydayness. Everydayness is the enemy. No search is possible. Perhaps there was a time when everydayness was not too strong and one could break its grip by brute strength. Now nothing breaks it—but disaster. Only once in my life was the grip of everydayness broken when I lay bleeding in a ditch. (145)

It was at that time that he had experienced two days of dreamless sleep (83-4), and he must be, as his father was, tempted to seek extinction, now that his moviegoing evasions no longer seem to work.

But then he acts like a stubborn infant:

> In a sudden rage and, as if I had been seized by a fit, I roll over and fall in a heap on the floor and lie shivering on the boards, worse off than the miserablest muskrat in the swamp. Nevertheless I vow: I'm a son of a bitch if I'll be defeated by everydayness. (145)

And indeed he would be a son of a bitch (goddess) if he succumbed to an alienation which she had caused. He resolves to resume the search that he has occasionally mentioned, the existential repetition (or quest or return), which ends, according to "The Man on the Train," "before the house of one's childhood" (96).

Such a resolution allows Binx to go back to sleep, a deep sleep, it may be inferred from his description of awakening:

> It starts as an evil turn of events. There is a sense of urgency. Something has to be done. Let us please do something about it. Then it is a color, a very bad color that needs tending to. Then a pain. But there is no use: it is a sound and it is out there in the world and nothing can be done about it. Awake. (146-7)

The description sounds more like a fetus trying not to be born or like a moviegoer at a movie with a bad projectionist. Then Binx is before the house of his childhood:

> The world is like milk: sky, water, savannah. The thin etherlike water vaporizes; tendrils of fog gather like smoke; a white shaft lies straight as a ruler over the marsh. (147)

As Binx listens to his stepfather going off to fish, he becomes aware of his isolation:

> The hull disappears into a white middle distance and the sound goes suddenly small as if the boat had run into cotton.
>
> A deformed live oak emerges from the whiteness, stands up in the air, like a tree in a Chinese print. Minutes pass. (147-8)

Binx can only wait:

> Behind me a screen door opens softly and my mother comes out on the dock with a casting rod . . . 'Hinhhonh,' she says in a yawn-sigh as wan and white as the morning. Her blouse is one of Roy's army shirts and not much too big for her large breasts. (148)

In fantasy Binx has pursued the mother-near-the-water during his entire narration, and now she stands before him, "her large breasts" lactating his world, like the Great Mother of old (Neumann 32) or like Juno, whose lactation created the Milky Way (Warner 196).

Binx pulls on his pants, to walk barefoot into "a cool milky world" (148):

> 'Isn't it mighty early for you!' Her voice is a tinkle over the water.
>
> My mother is easy and affectionate with me. Now we may speak together. It is the early morning and our isolation in the great white marsh.
>
> 'Can I fix you some breakfast?'
>
> 'No'm. I'm not hungry.' Our voices go ringing around the empty room of the morning.

Surely it comes as a surprise that Binx would refuse her gesture, for Binx has been speaking, ever since his memory of the movie out by Lake Pontchartrain (5), of the empty room that represents the womb and of the whiteness of the water locale and of the empty movie screen (soon to be discussed) that represents the breast. But

Binx's next statement explains his reason for declining: "Still she puts me off" (149). Binx seems to realize that she will be his nurse no better than she was his father's.

Binx notes that his mother "veers away from intimacy" (149), would prefer to talk about fishing. When he says that he does not like to fish, she replies, "You're just like your father." Binx stretches "out at full length," nestling his "head on a two-by-four," as if it were a mother's arm: "It is possible to squint into the rising sun and at the same time see my mother spangled in rainbows" (149-50), like a promise. The description of nursing by Kristeva offered earlier should be recalled.

Binx needs both nourishment and news. As if to tease him in both his desires, his mother tells of his father's one successful fishing trip, when he caught a sac au lait, so named by the Louisiana French in an attempt to pronounce Choctaw *sakli*, their name for the fish known in English as *trout* (Mathews, 1438). That *sakli* became *sac au lait* may speak volumes about Gallic psychosexual development. For Binx's father the fish was no more a mamma than his wife would be. In time, Binx's mother turns the conversation to her father, who also was not a fisherman, though "[h]e owned a fleet of trawlers at Golden Meadow. But did he love pretty girls. Till his dying day" (155). Still squinting "up at her through the rainbows," Binx asks, "Does it last that long?" Her reply is sharp and conclusive: "Don't you get risqué with me! This is your mother you're talking to and not one of your little hotsy-totsies." Apparently admitting defeat, Binx concludes, "Fishing is poor" (159), and there will be no "penis in the vagina" or "foetus in the uterus" at all.

What has been going on here? It should be remembered that Binx is constructing his narrative at least a year after the fact (for a violation of the "virtual present" of the narrative proper, see the anticipation of the "catastrophe Monday night" just as Binx and Kate arrive in Chicago on Monday morning, 201). It should be kept in mind, too, that Binx uses in his narrative either the same terms—rotation, (aesthetic) repetition—or closely equivalent terms—"malaise" for alienation, "search" for existential repetition—of the psychological system discussed in "The Man on the Train"; thus he implies that he is basing his interpretation and description of his earlier behavior on that system. Further, he makes in his narrative the same basic distinction that is made by "The Man on the Train"; for his narrative, the "vertical search" names the objective-empirical technique and the "horizontal search" (70) names the alienated response (and its putative deliverances). And, also, since he mentions

Freud's *Interpretation of Dreams* in connection with his teenage curiosity and his mother's aloofness (138), he implies a long and close sensitivity to psychoanalytic literature, especially as it might benefit him. Finally, since he identifies himself as a "moviegoer" (109) and uses moviegoing and movie lore to illustrate his psychological theories and his impersonations, he implies a full knowledge of the psychoanalysis of moviegoing, as summarized in such recent studies as Robert Eberwein's *Film and The Dream Screen* (1984) and Judith Mayne's *Private Novels, Public Films* (1988). With these considerations in mind, it is quite possible that Binx has relied upon a psychoanalytic theory formulated by Bertram Lewin to structure his narrative, especially the scene between his mother and himself on the dock. But even if Binx is not familiar with Lewin's research, it can, nevertheless, be used to gloss his mental and physical behavior.

Lewin introduced his theory in "Sleep, the Mouth, and the Dream Screen." His curiosity was aroused by Freud's comment in *The Interpretation of Dreams* that a wish to sleep is "the prime reason for all dreaming, the dream being the great guardian of sleep" (419). Lewin was also pondering M. J. Eisler's assertion "that sleep [is] a regressive phenomenon, a return to hypothetical preoral or apnoeic stage, such as might be imagined for the unborn child" (419). Then a patient in session told him: "I had my dream all ready for you; but while I was lying here looking at it, it turned over away from me, rolled up, and rolled away from me—over and over like two tumblers" (420). Lewin was inspired to conceive of the "dream screen."

Lewin later reported, in "Inferences from the Dream Screen," that the analogy between the dream process and the moviegoing experience occurred to him immediately (226). (This is the same analogy that Susanne Langer was to formulate later, except that she reversed the terms: it is also the same analogy that is undeveloped in Julia Kristeva's description of the nursing event.)[8] As refined and developed by Lewin and other analysts—Charles Rycroft, Joseph Kepecs, Gert Heilbrunn, Mark Kanzer, Angel Garma, L. Bryce Boyer, and Carel van der Heide—the following model of the dreamer as moviegoer is widely used.

When a baby nurses, it wishes to nurse to gratification, then to drop into a dreamless, regressive sleep. The last visual impression that it reaches before sleeping is the huge blank breast that is not far enough distant even to be perceived as an object separate from the ego. The baby therefore internalizes the breast as a blank dream, a blank screen with nothing on it. This internalization is not abandoned in time. As the ego develops, manifest content dreams —unconscious wishes that threaten to awaken the sleeper—are projected onto the dream screen, but that screen is ordinarily not recalled when the manifest dream is recalled. But as some people begin to awaken, the ego sometimes has the experience of seeing the dream screen—on which is projected a visual dream—receding, losing its flat appearance, assuming a smaller curved shape. The experience of the dream screen seems more prevalent among those dreamers who have deep oral fixations. Such dreamers also have fantasies of intrauterine regression, but there is also the possibility of a conflicting psychic energy, a death wish. Thus some such dreamers fight sleep, to the extent that "the tensions may be carried over into a dreamlike awakening in which the identifications and the instinctual goals remain confused" (Kanzer, 519). In "Reconsideration of the Dream Screen" Lewin offers a composite of reports of the dream screen:

> The whitish, cloudy, endless wall is the breast or the ghost of a breast—thus sensed by the diplopic amblyopic baby, with its weak powers of accommodation and its confused depth and color perceptions. Notably the screen equivalent in such dreams is of badly defined thickness and consistency; it is thick or fluid, dark or whitish or milky, out of focus—indeed questionably visual at all. . . . (183)

What does the model of the dream screen have to say about Binx's narrative? With his first description of moviegoing, Binx shows that a movie theater re-presents his fantasy of regression to the womb. When he comes out of his moviegoing, he generally heads for water, another image of intrauterine flight. Having denied the reality of his biological mother, he has split his fantasy figure: Mrs. Schexnaydre is the "bad mother," while each new secretary is the "good mother," as long as she represents pure possibility. Binx's oral fixation shows his need to nurse to satisfaction, so that he could sleep soundly (and thus see the dream screen) instead of the manifest content (such as the skaters in Central Park) which haunts his head. He suffers, instead, from dream disturbance, even as he fears relaxing his fragile grip on his ego so that he could sleep, for the regression might then be fatal.

In the scene at the fishing camp Binx suffers from dreaming, then makes a first effort to resist. Then he dreams the dream screen (146-7), even tries to prevent "color" and "sound" from occurring on the screen, thus waking him. The subsequent whiteness imagery indicates that the dream screen lingers, even as his mother appears through the "screen" (148)—it will be recalled that Binx described his "father crashing through the screen door, . . . his eyes criss-crossed by fatigue and by the sadness of these glimmering dawns" (85), such as Binx is now seeing. Then, by stretching out on the dock, Binx positions himself as the child at the breast of the nurse. His rejection of her offer to make his breakfast reveals that he is coming to the realization that she simply cannot be a gratifying mother. He is progressing from a dependence upon ideal internal objects toward a more realistic response to things as they are, thus showing ego development.[9]

This is not to say that Binx's recovery will be quick and/or complete. On the way back to New Orleans on Sunday afternoon, he falls back into his rotational fantasy, seeking "the thickest and innerest part of Sharon's thigh" (166), which is just a *frisson* from fusion, fantasy's focus:

> She bats me away with new vigor.
>
> 'Son, don't you mess with me.'
>
> 'Very well, I won't,' I say gloomily, as willing not to mess with her as mess with her, to tell the truth.
>
> 'That's all right. You come here.'
>
> 'I'm here.'
>
> She gives me a kiss. 'I got your number, son. But that's all right. You're a good old boy. You really tickle me.' She's been talking to my mother. 'Now you tend to your business and get me on home.'
>
> 'Why?'
>
> 'I have to meet someone.'

Before they had started to the beach, Sharon had asked Binx, "Is Miss Cutrer any kin to you" (118), already suspecting that the romantic role of a Binx secretary is to be a temporary, not a permanent hire. Now, having talked with the real mother, who has been telling Binx for years that he should marry Kate (155), this hotsy-totsy realizes that she had better be getting out to "meet someone" of her own.

His fantasy of attainment having thus been rebuffed, Binx goes to the home of his Aunt Emily in the Garden District—certainly no garden district for him—there to suffer from his loss of sleep "during the past week" (182). Then, with Kate, he literally becomes "the man on the train," directed by his Uncle Jules to attend a convention in Chicago. His drowsiness had been but a prelude to his condition on the train:

> The drowsiness returns. It is unwelcome. I recognize it as the sort of fitful twilight which has come over me of late, a twilight where waking dreams are dreamed and sleep never comes. (188)

The sleep that never comes is also the penis that never comes. Back at Aunt Emily's, Sam Yerger had asked the departing Binx, "Brother Andy, is you getting much" (183). The fact is, that for all Binx's elaborate Don Juan behavior, he mentions not one orgasm, that experience of fusion that he seeks through regression. Significantly, Binx alternates looking out the window and looking over the shoulder of his reading neighbor, both actions mirroring what is on his mind:

> We pause at an advertisement of a Bourbon Street nightclub which is a picture of a dancer with an oiled body. Her triceps arch forward like a mare's. For a second we gaze heavy-lidded and pass on. Now he finds what he wants. . . . Dreaming at his shoulder, I can make out no more than
>
> In order to deepen and enrich the marital—It is a counseling column which I too read faithfully. (188-9)

As the "train sways through the swamp" (189), Binx is miserable:

> Staying awake is a kind of sickness and sleep is forever guarded against by a dizzy dutiful alertness. Waking wide-eyed dreams come as fitfully as swampfire.

His condition like that earlier described by Mark Kanzer as "a dreamlike awakening," Binx has a waking dream of the sexologists Dean, whom he had seen at a Canal Street book-signing of their collaboration *Technique in Marriage*, one technique of which begins: "Now with a tender regard for your partner remove your hand from the nipple and gently manipulate . . ." (191). At this point in the life of the moviegoer/man-on-the-train, a remark by Joseph Kepecs, in "A Waking Screen Analogous to the Dream Screen," is appropriate: "It is quite likely that many people are unable to perceive the real world clearly because between it and themselves they interpose a phantom of the maternal breast through which everything else is seen" (171). This scene once again confirms that the existential concerns of "The Man on the Train" are the psychosexual concerns of *The Moviegoer*.

Kate herself is in a serious crisis, part of a long-term condition that may have originated in deprivation of the object (110-111), for her mother, it is to be inferred, died before Kate was three years old. Binx implies that they share the same condition, even as they share her roomette on the train. He observes the dream screen:

> Outside a square of yellow light flees along an embankment, falls away to the woods and fields, comes roaring back good as new. Suddenly a perky head pops up. Kate is leaning forward hugging herself.

He observes her observing the dream screen:

> She is back at her window, moving her hand to see it move in the flying yellow square.

He concludes:

> We hunch up knee to knee and nose to nose like the two devils on the Rorschach card.[10] (192)

With such mutuality of misery, they begin to discuss marriage, a subject which has come up between them before (116). Since Kate is as alienated as Binx, it follows that she too has been dreaming of orgasms as fusion (199). They try, therefore, to consummate their relationship, hoping for deep, dreamless sleep: Binx imagines himself dispatching Kate into "as sweet a sleep as ever Scarlett enjoyed the morning of Rhett's return" (200). But "flesh poor flesh" failed them. Then Kate imagines herself as Ophelia (210), undone by another mother's boy, according to Freud.

Despite their sexual failure, Binx is developing the strength to express his love for Kate, who looks after him (201) much as a mother hen, "with many a cluck and much fuss" (202). He suffers not even "two seconds of malaise" (204). Then, in a bar on the Loop, Binx looks at Kate:

> . . . I see her plain, see plain for the first time since I lay wounded in a ditch and watched an Oriental finch scratching around in the leaves—a quiet little body she is, a tough little city Celt; no, more of a Rachel really, a dark little Rachel bound home to Brooklyn on the IRT. I give her a pat on the leg. (206)

Kepecs' comment about the "phantom of the maternal breast through which everything else is seen" is appropriate here. By calling Kate a Rachel, Binx may only mean that she is like a Jew, whom he has earlier epitomized as the alienated person (88-9), but there is the possibility that he is thinking of the Rachel who wept for her children. He knows that he needs that kind of wife who can feed his maternal deprivation. For once, he is free of the desire that is symptomatic of his nostalgia (207).

Even a visit to the home of some Wilmette suburbanites fails to dismay the couple:

> Back to the Loop where we dive into the mother and Urwomb of all moviehouses—an Aztec mortuary of funeral urns and glyphs thronged with the spirit-presences of another day, William Powell and George Brent and Patsy Kelly and Charley Chase, the best friends of my childhood—and see a movie called *The Young Philadelphians*. Kate holds my hand tightly in the dark. (211)

Looking back from his post-recovery vantage point, Binx now knows what the movie theater had meant to him before, the locus of all his repetitional fantasies, and can name it for what it had been. Ernest Becker says:

> The dream mode, like the cinema, brings fantasied fulfillment in a shallowly lived present. The shortcomings of our world are remedied in fancy allowing one to transpose the body of his wife into that of his favorite movie star. (39)

In his childhood loneliness, Binx had sought fantasy friends in the movie theater, the very locus of loss. But now he has found a fellow inhabitant in the city of love (as the movie title indicates); he even offers a synopsis of the movie, for he now realizes that it had foreshadowed his destiny:

> Paul Newman is an idealistic young fellow who is disillusioned and becomes cynical and calculating. But in the end he recovers his ideals. (211)

Then Paul is worthy of his Christian name—and so is Binx.

The forces of the past do not, however, give up their hold so easily. In his drowsy and dazed condition, Binx had neglected to tell his Aunt Emily of Kate's decision to go to Chicago with him. Outraged, she summons her nephew back to New Orleans for judgment. Her wrath is terrible, for, with one question, she reveals that she has absolutely no comprehension of her nephew's desperate condition ("What do you think is the purpose of life—to go to the movies and dally with every girl that comes along" [226]), for both behaviors originate in his mother-loss.[11]

Dismissed, Binx sees no future but Mrs. Schexnaydre's basement—but Kate tells him to wait there for her. While he waits, he is convinced that he will despair like his father; the future looks so bleak that he can only "fall prey to desire" (228), become once again a captive of nostalgia. He even tries to contact Sharon, to revive his fantasy quest for the "oceanic feeling"; standing in an "evil-smelling" telephone booth, he is mocked by a piece of playground equipment: "*Iii-oorr* goes the ocean wave, its struts twinkling in the golden light, its skirt swaying to and fro like a young dancing girl" (231), like the vision of Aphrodite presented by Sharon in the golden light on the beach. But, having found a "someone," Sharon is not at home; rather Binx talks to her roommate, Joyce, for whom he has harbored rotatory yearnings: "I've been wanting to meet you for some time" (229). But even she could be mocking Binx, for she replies, "The Lord of Misrule reigned yesterday . . ." (230) [on Shrove Tuesday]. As Ian Suttie explains, the Lord of Misrule is a late survivor of the young male lover-victim who was sacrificed each spring in the Great Mother rites (130).

But then Kate proves loyal, does not abandon him as his fantasy-mother Sharon had. Kate's savior role had been foreshadowed earlier, when Sam Yerger tells Binx that when he saw Kate he said to himself: My God, . . . there goes Natasha Rostov" (171). As Paul Friedrich notes: " . . . the striking thing about Natasha in *War and Peace* is her drastic shift from being an erotic adolescent to being a Slavic *Urmutter* . . ." (182-3). Since Binx has read "the novel of novels" (69), he should have had a little more confidence in Kate. At the playground they reaffirm their decision to marry. Such is the restoration of his spirit that he sees a sign of God's grace—a black man emerging from a Catholic church with his forehead marked with ashes—and converts, achieves an existential repetition.

In the "Epilogue" Binx reviews the events which have occurred since he and Kate decided to marry. The June marriage and his September entry into medical school indicate that he has escaped the hold of mother-loss and accepted the role at which his father had foundered, thus transcended both the preoedipal and oedipal conditions that had caused his psychic dysfunction. And since both actions were *doing the right thing*, in Aunt Emily's eyes, even if she does not understand them, he is reconciled to her. The next Mardi Gras, Uncle Jules, at the Boston Club, suffered a second heart attack, which proved fatal. Then in May his half-brother Lonnie died of a "massive virus infection" (237). Kate still suffers from severe anxiety. Binx refuses to say anything about himself—directly—for existential repetitions cannot be transmitted in literature. But he has endured the ordeal and received the four boons of reward described by Joseph Campbell—sacred marriage, father atonement, apotheosis, and elixir theft (246). He does not mention the movies (or screens, either dream or door). Nor does he mention his old hankering for Central Park; instead, he reveals that on the day of Lonnie's death, he took his brothers and sisters to ride the train in Audubon Park (240). Binx is still the man on the train, but his destination now is the City of God.

Notes

[1] *In Feeling and Form* Langer speaks of the likeness of cinema to dream and of the "virtual present" (412), both ideas essential to the technique of *The Moviegoer*. That Percy had closely read *Feeling and Form* is apparent from his review of it, "Symbol as Need," *Thought* 29 (Autumn 1954): 381-90.

[2] See my essay, "'The Parent in the Percept' in *The Last Gentleman*" for a discussion of psychically-impaired visualization in Percy's second published novel.

[3] Percy's essay "The Man on the Train," *Partisan Review* 23 (Fall 1956): 478-94, with its discussion of moviegoing and his psychology of alienation, was an essential preparation for the writing of and is an essential preparation for the reading of *The Moviegoer*.

[4] Otto: "Poets after Homer call [Aphrodite] 'golden' and speak of her as the 'smiling' . . . goddess" (97). See my "The Moviegoer Dates the Love Goddess," for Binx Bolling's visualization of Sharon as Marilyn Monroe, who was the personification of Aphrodite for the 1960-1961 "virtual present" of *The Moviegoer*.

[5] See my "Walker Percy's *The Moviegoer*: the Cinema as Cave," for a discussion of Binx Bolling's scientistic education.

[6] See Firestone: "When deprived of love-food, an infant experiences considerable anxiety and pain and attempts to compensate by sucking its thumb and providing self-nourishment in various ways. At this point in its development, a baby is able to create the illusion of the breast. An infant who feels empty and starved emotionally relies increasingly on this fantasy for gratification. And, indeed, this process provides partial relief. In working with regressed schizophrenic patients, my colleagues and I observed that some had visions and dreams of white hazes, snow, and the like, sometimes representing the wish for milk and nourishment. One patient described to me a white breast that he saw, and when I asked what came out of it, he said 'Pictures.' Thus, fantasy may eventually become 'more real' to the seriously disturbed person than does experience in the 'real' environment" (37-38).

[7] For an object-relations study of Housman, see Wolfenstein.

[8] See Esman: First he offers an account of a session: "About three months after he began psychotherapy, Tommy reported that he had gone with his father to a baseball game the previous Sunday. They had little to say to one another, their principal communication consisting of Tommy's request for ice cream and his father's preemptory refusal to buy it for him. That night the child had the following dream:

> I was sitting in a movie theater, or someplace. There was sort of a screen, and baseballs were coming out of it toward me. There was a man there who was catching the balls and deflecting them to everyone else, so I couldn't get any."

Esman makes this interpretation: "The dream reported here appears to exemplify the dream screen concept in all respects. The day residue is an experience of oral deprivation in a profoundly oral fixated boy, in whom depression and overeating represent desperate attempts at restitution for gross early deprivations. The frustrating person in the dream is a direct representation of the reality figure. Aside from its obvious transference implications, the latent content of the dream appears to be: 'My father repeatedly deprives me of the breast and milk that I so desperately want. Only by directly representing the breast and its longed-for solace can I remain asleep.' Thus, the dream is seen to have oedipal and preoedipal content; it serves the oral regression that is the principal defensive measure at this boy's disposal against the intense rage evoked by the experience of deprivation" (250-51).

[9] See Boyer: "Rycroft's patient (personal communication 1959) 'was in a state of "narcissistic identification" since (1) he had withdrawn interest from external objects, (2) he was preoccupied with an introject, and (3) he identified himself with this introject.' The analysand presented dream screen phenomena at a time when an object relationship was developing. Rycroft considered the most significant aspect of the appearance of the screen phenomenon to be that it marked a shift from narcissistic identification with the internal object to turning toward an external object. He concluded that the phenomenon of the dream screen represents, in addition to the fulfillment of the wish to sleep at the mother's breast, an attempt in the course of the analysis of reestablish an object relationship with the mother via the transference" (48). Through his self-analysis (i.e. his narrative) Binx is describing his success in shifting from an internal object to an external object.

[10] It is tempting to think that Binx alludes to Rorschach Plate VII, which, as Booth—Percy's second psychoanalyst—acknowledges, many Rorschach psychologists interpret as the "mother card" (97).

[11] This scene reflects a very important aspect of Walker Percy's psychodrama. The character "Aunt Emily" is based on Percy's adoptive father (his father's first cousin) William Alexander Percy, an unmarried man who seems never to have had a heterosexual relationship. Thus his validity as a father-figure may have been undercut in Percy's mind, as the gender change of the character might suggest. Percy's biographer Tolson cites the paper by Janet Rioch, Percy's first psychoanalyst, which, he believes, discusses Percy's aborted analysis (140-43) and which, I believe, supports my inferences. I suggest that it was the aborted analyses which destined Percy to work through his self-analysis in fiction.

Works Cited

Balint, Michael. *Primary Love and Psycho-Analytic Technique*. London: Hogarth, 1952.

Becker, Ernest. *The Revolution in Psychiatry*. New York: Free Press of Glencoe, 1964.

Booth, Gotthard. *The Cancer Epidemic: Shadow of the Conquest of Nature*. New York: Edwin Mellen, 1979.

Boyer, L. Bryce. *The Regressed Patient*. New York: Jason Aronson, 1983.

Brazelton, T. Berry, and Bertrand G. Cramer. *The Earliest Relationship*. Reading, MA: Addison-Wesley, 1989.

Campbell, Joseph. *The Hero with a Thousand Faces*. New York: Meridian, 1956.

Eberwein, Robert T. *Film and the Dream Screen*. Princeton: Princeton UP, 1984.

Esman, Aaron H. "The Dream Screen in an Adolescent." *The Psychoanalytic Quarterly* 31 (1962): 250-51.

Ferenczi, Sandor. *Thalassa*. Albany: The Psychoanalytic Quarterly, 1938.

Firestone, Robert W. *The Fantasy Bond*. New York: Human Sciences Press, 1985.

Flugel, J. C. *The Psycho-Analytic Study of the Family*. London: Hogarth, 1960.

Freud, Sigmund. *A General Introduction to Psychoanalysis*. New York: Pocket, 1953.

Friedrich, Paul. *The Meaning of Aphrodite*. Chicago: U of Chicago P, 1978.

Greenberg, Harvey R. *The Movies on Your Mind*. New York: Saturday Review Press, 1975.

Harding, M. Esther. *The 'I' and the 'Not-I'*. Princeton: Princeton UP, 1965.

Johnson, Timothy W. "Holiday." *Magill's Survey of Cinema*, First Series, II, ed. Frank N. Magill. Englewood Cliffs, NJ: Salem House, 1980. 758-61.

Kanzer, Mark. "Observations on Blank Dreams with Orgasms." *The Psychoanalytic Quarterly* 23 (1954): 511-20.

Kepecs, Joseph. "A Waking Screen Analogous to the Dream Screen." *The Psychoanalytic Quarterly* 21 (1952): 167-71.

Langer, Susanne. *Feeling and Form*. New York: Scribner's, 1953.

Lawson, Lewis A. "The Moviegoer Dates the Love Goddess." *The Southern Quarterly* 33 (Fall 1994): 7-25.

—. 'The Parent in the Percept' in *The Last Gentleman*." *Mississippi Quarterly* 46 (1992-93): 39-59.

—. "Walker Percy's The Moviegoer: the Cinema as Cave." *Southern Studies* 19 (1980): 331-54.

Lewin, Bertram D. *The Image and the Past*. New York: International Universities Press, 1968.

—. "Inferences from the Dream Screen." *International Journal of Psychoanalysis* 29 (1948): 224-30.

—. "Reconsideration of the Dream Screen." *The Psychoanalytic Quarterly* 22 (1953): 174-99.

—. "Sleep, the Mouth, and the Dream Screen." *The Psychoanalytic Quarterly* 15 (1946): 419-34.

Mathews, Mitford M. *A Dictionary of Americanisms on Historical Principles*. Chicago: U of Chicago P, 1951.

Mayne, Judith. *Private Novels, Public Films*. Athens: U of Georgia P, 1988.

Muensterberger, Werner. "Between Reality and Fantasy." *Between Reality and Fantasy*. Eds. Simon A. Grolnick and Leonard Barkin. New York: Jason Aronson, 1978. 3-13.

Neumann, Erich. *The Origins and History of Consciousness*. Princeton: Princeton UP, 1954.

Otto, Walter. *The Homeric Gods*. Boston: Beacon, 1954.

Percy, Walker. "From Facts to Fiction." *The Washington Post Book Week* 25 December 1966: 6, 9.

—. "The Man on the Train." *The Message in the Bottle*. New York: Farrar, Straus and Giroux, 1975. 83-100.

—. *The Moviegoer*. New York: Noonday, 1967.

—. "Symbol as Need." *The Message in the Bottle*. 288-97.

Person, Ethel Spector. *Dreams of Love and Fateful Encounters*. New York: Norton, 1988.

Romanyshyn, Robert. *Psychological Life*. Austin: U of Texas P, 1982.

Rosen, George. "Percussion and Nostalgia." *Journal of the History of Medicine and Allied Sciences* 27 (1972): 448-50.

Suttie, Ian. *The Origins of Love and Hate*. New York: Matrix House, 1966.

Tolson, Jay. *Pilgrim in the Ruins*. New York: Simon and Schuster, 1992.

Warner, Marina. *Alone of All Her Sex*. New York: Alfred A. Knopf, 1976.

Wolfenstein, Martha. "The Image of the Lost Parent." *The Psychoanalytic Study of the Child* 28 (1973): 433-56.

Gesture and Style in *The Moviegoer*

Emory Elliott

> My first idea was the building itself. It looks like a miniature bank with its Corinthian pilasters, portico and iron scrolls over the windows. The firm's name, Cutrer, Klostermann & Lejier is lettered in Gothic and below in smaller letters, the names of the Boston mutual funds we represent. It looks far more conservative than the modern banks in Gentilly. It announces to the world: modern methods are no doubt excellent but here is good old-fashioned stability, but stability with imagination. A little bit of old New England with a Creole flavor. The Parthenon façade cost twelve thousand dollars but commissions have doubled. The young man you see inside is clearly the soul of integrity; he asks no more than to be allowed to plan your future. This is true. This is all I ask.[1]

In the midst of the existential lament of John-Jack-Binx-Rollo-Bolling, the humor of this passage may not at first be apparent. Like an image out of a novel by Fenimore Cooper depicting the comic amalgam of styles in America, the façade blends elements of European and American regional architecture to convey a permanent, ambiguous advertising slogan of puritanical austerity and classical splendor. Behind the façade lurks a paradoxical confidence man/pilgrim who does not believe himself to be the soul of *financial* integrity and stability that he advertises but who does

---

This essay was previously published in *Revista de Estudos Germânicos* [Universidade Federal de Minas Gerais, Belo Horizonte, Brazil], 9 (December 1988), 30-37, and is reprinted here by the generous permission of Junia de Castro Magalhaes Alves, co-editor.

yearn for *psychological* integrity. Encumbered in his search for spiritual meaning and self-knowledge by the very jumble of cultural fragments projected on the façade, Binx does wish ironically on a more profound and idealistic level to plan people's lives, and he waits to plan lives—his own and others. But like his literary forebearers, the unreliable narrators Miles Coverdale, Jake Barnes, and Nick Carraway, and Melville's Pierre and the failed Southern searcher Quentin Compson, Binx may be unable to escape the double-bond of narcissism and self-deception which makes him a self-righteous critic of his world who employs irony to deny the implications of his own participation and responsibility. Or like another set of literary predecessors, Huck Finn, Ike McCaslin, Warren's Jack Burden, and Ellison's Invisible Man, he may be able to cast off some of the layers of the facade of the Puritan, Enlightenment, Euro-American Southern self to discover some remnant of a human soul worthy of a future.

This comic passage points to the conflict between the public and private man which is at the thematic center of *The Moviegoer* and of the critical controversies surrounding the text. The problem of the book as it is usually posed is what sort of resolution does Binx achieve at the end of the novel? After all of his high-minded talk of malaise, everydayness, cultural collapse, and the need to search for new values and a personal spiritual calling, Binx's situation at the conclusion is ambiguous at best or is at worst a sentimental acceptance of his Aunt Emily's imposed mission. Of his spiritual seeking, Binx says in the Epilogue, "I have not the inclination to say much on the subject" (187) and he retreats behind the hard-boiled language of a Hemingway anti-hero: "much too late to edify or do much of anything except plant a foot in the right place as the opportunity presents itself—if indeed asskicking is properly distinguished from edification" (187-88). He seems to have advanced only slightly from the soldier his aunt told him to be when he was eight to the rank of drill sergeant. After seeming to prepare his heart, and the reader, for his spiritual conversion, he is now "shy" on the subject of religion. He appears embarrassed and awkward about all that has gone before and quick to complete his manuscript: "Reticence, therefore, hardly having a place in a document of this kind, it seems as good a time as any to make an end" (188). A reader may well feel that Binx's Celestial Railroad ride from New Orleans to Chicago has merely come full circle to bring its pilgrim-seeker to an unexpected but hardly transformed station in life. Such ambiguity has led many critics to seek out the real

Walker Percy himself to ask him what this all means.[2]

When critics prepare for these interviews, they learn the essential biographical facts. Percy had a tragic childhood. His father committed suicide when Walker was thirteen, and his mother died in an automobile accident when he was fifteen. He was raised by a second cousin, William Alexander Percy, a "bachelor-poet-lawyer-planter" who imparted to Walker the Greek-Roman Stoic vision expressed by Aunt Emily in *The Moviegoer*. Walker went to the University of North Carolina to study chemistry and to Columbia University medical school. During two bouts with tuberculosis, he read extensively in French and Russian literature and philosophy. In the late 1940s he married, converted to Roman Catholicism, settled permanently in Covington, Louisiana, and began to write essays about alienation, existentialism, malaise, and the failure of Christianity in the modern world. He published his first novel *The Moviegoer* in 1961.

Noting the obvious autobiographical elements in the novel, critics often assume that Binx's resolution parallels Percy's own quest for answers. Like Percy, Binx is a young man who sees through the sham of public rhetoric and discovers the meaning of alienation, malaise, and nausea. Turning aside from the false values of materialism and empiricism, Binx, like Percy, was led by European philosophy to discover a new sense of purpose upon which to base a radically new plan for life.[3]

The problem with this reading, however, is that it is not borne out by the text, especially that of the final chapter and epilogue. It also overlooks another dimension of Percy's work that he himself sometimes mentions but that criticism has tended to slight—his debt to American writers. At various times, Percy has said that he admires the works of Poe, Hawthorne, Melville, Twain, Hemingway, Faulkner, O'Connor, Welty, Ellison, and Wright, and he dots his works with literary allusions and with references to American history and popular culture. In fact, alertness to the many allusions to American predecessors can reveal some quite delightful parodies of the styles of other writers. *The Moviegoer* opens with allusions to the opening of *Absalom, Absalom!* where Quentin is summoned by a note to visit Miss Rosa Coldfield and Mr. Sartalamaccia's story of the hunting party at Roaring Camp recalls Faulkner's *The Bear*, including the breaking of Binx's watch, which alludes to both works. When he tells of how Judge Anse (remember Anse Bundren in *As I Lay Dying*) ordered him, like Thomas Sutpen, to build him a lodge, Mr. Sartalamaccia "waits until the words, the very words, speak themselves" (177). And, of course, when they speak, they appear in italics. These humorous evocations of America and American literary traditions are not merely part of a veneer of Americanism that Percy lays over the philosophical, European core of his work, in the way that Binx employs the gestures of movie actors to mask his inner emptiness. Instead, style and gesture are an integral part of the work as a whole, and call attention to the subtle forms of communication, both verbal and non-verbal, that operate between the characters. Body movement, physical mannerisms, silences, and shifts in tone often impart coded messages between characters and may suggest to the reader other possible explanations of the novel's resolution.

Close attention to the functions of style and gesture in *The Moviegoer* not only provides a key to the novel's ending, but it also can help us account for the intricacy of Binx's relationships with Kate and Aunt Emily and explain the meaning of his comment in the Epilogue that "both women find me comical and laugh a good deal at my expense" (187). Percy himself has been accused by several critics of sexism, and he does admit that his female characters do not fare too well.[4] However, the women in *The Moviegoer* may fare better than it at first may appear.

In order to see the roles of Emily and Kate in the novel clearly, it is necessary to make distinction between the narrator and the narrative audience he addresses and the author and his authorial audience. Binx makes certain assumptions about social and cultural attitudes that he believes he shares with his projected narrative audience. For example, Binx assumes that his readers share his liberal attitudes on race and social class and are dismayed, with him, at the racist and aristocratic attitudes Aunt Emily exhibits in her final outburst about the decline of the old South. While it is possible that Percy may also make that assumption about his authorial audience, he makes other assumptions of which Binx is never aware. Percy's literary allusions and parodies of the style of other American writers, for example, are signals to the author's audience of another level of communication at work to which Binx is not privileged.

Once the reader begins to distinguish between these two narrative voices, he or she may also recognize other elements of the narrative to which Binx is blind. He never records a conscious recognition of the fact, for example, that he never really proposed marriage to Kate but that she transformed his suggestion that she might visit him to watch television into a proposal upon which they finally both act. Binx's belief that Kate is mentally disturbed to the point of not being able to control *her* life may prevent him from seeing the degree to which she controls *his* life. Actually, his life is much more controlled by Emily and Kate than he realizes. The ways in which Kate subtly uses style and gesture to control Binx's destiny are immediately evident because they are never apparent to Binx himself. Focus upon the function of style and gesture within the text reveals the fallacy of the autobiographical interpretation of *The Moviegoer* and suggests that Binx is hardly the godlike prime mover that Kate proclaims him to be.

It is at first perhaps hard to imagine that Binx himself could be the victim of another's use of style, for he is so conscious of using externals to represent a chosen image of the self in order to achieve his desires. The most humorous and revealing example of his process of self-projection is his experience in choosing a car. He adheres to the Madison Avenue association of cars with sex. "You say it is a simple thing surely . . . to pick up a good-looking woman and head for the beach on the first fine day of the year. So say the newspaper poets. Well, it's not such a simple thing . . ." (99). "The car itself is all important." Initially, he chose a car that fit the image he wished to present of himself as a reliable young businessman. But on his first date with Marcia in his Dodge Ram Six sedan, he "discovered to my dismay that my fine new Dodge was a regular incubator of malaise." He recalls, "We sat frozen in a gelid amiability. Our cheeks ached from smiling. . . . Marcia and I returned to New Orleans defeated by the malaise. It was weeks before we ventured out again" (100).

Confident that his sexual failure here (which parallels similar failures with Sharon and even Kate) was the fault of a car rather than himself, Binx buys a symbol of sexual potency, a red MG: "My little red MG . . . is immune to the malaise. You have no idea what happiness Marcia and I experienced as soon as we found ourselves spinning along the highway in this bright little beetle. We looked at each other in astonishment: the malaise was gone!" (100). When Binx sets out to seduce Sharon—who, he says, will bring him the greatest "happiness" yet—Percy has his narrator describe their ride in the MG in the imagery of Binx's movie fantasies. The comic linking Binx's hyperbole of the car in battle to the serious notion of cultural malaise signals the gap between the author and his narrator:

> For the stakes were very high. Either very great happiness lay in store for us, or malaise past all conceiving [Freudian slips on Binx's part? Intentional puns on Percy's part?]. . . . I spin along the precipice with the black-

> est malaise below and the greenest of valleys ahead. . . . [I]t seems to me that I catch a whiff of malaise. A little tongue of hellfire licks at our heels and the MG jumps ahead, roaring like a bomber through the sandy pine barrens and across Bay St. Louis. (101)

Binx assumes that the audience of his document shares his belief in the power of the material object to symbolize his sexual potency and attract Sharon to him, just as he had assumed that the building in Gentilly had brought him business. In the debate between Isabel Archer and Madame Merle in *The Portrait of a Lady* (a book alluded to through Percy's choice of "Merle" as the name for Kate's psychiatrist), Binx clearly sides with Merle that one's physical objects are an expression of oneself. But just as Gilbert Osmond's house and Binx's office building may present a deceptive façade, so too the gloss of the MG conceals sexual timidity and even impotence. Binx fails to note the contradiction in his theory about the MG's immunity when he and Sharon returned from the failed weekend and "the MG becomes infested with malaise" (133). When Sharon rejects his last desperate overture of his hand on her thigh with her firm "'Son, don't you mess with me,'" he reports: "'Very well, I won't, I say gloomily, as willing not to mess with her as mess with her, to tell the truth" (134). Kate says earlier that Binx is "'Colder [than she]. Cold as the grave'" (70). Sharon, having discovered herself to be a victim of false advertising rather than malaise, rushes back to renew her affair with the man she now intends to marry and over whom Binx expected to triumph. Kate, on the other hand, patiently persists in her own search of the real Binx and in the process to prepare him, not for grace, but for herself.

In spite of his MG, like bravados about his affairs with his secretaries, it is evident that Binx fears women, needs to feel in control in his relations with them, and finds it painfully difficult to communicate with women on a serious level. As he admits at the outset, his affairs with Marcia and Linda were superficial and ended in "telephone conversations . . . made up mostly of long silences" (15). In such silence he is not unlike his father, who left the marital bed to sleep in the back yard and who took ten-mile hikes alone. When Binx, who like Melville's Pierre is also on a search for his father, asks his mother if his father was a good husband, she answers that "' . . . he was a good walker'" (123). Lacking a strong self-image as a man, the way that he can conceive of himself with women is by invoking his fantasies of different movie actors and imitating their language and gestures. While he claims to be attracted to the Amazon type of woman with a helmet-like Prince Val haircut whom he sees on the bus and says mockingly that "[m]ost men are afraid of them" (17), he does not approach the girl even when he detects an inviting smile. Instead, he becomes absorbed by his thoughts of the search. Only Kate is able to reach him, and this is because she knows his secret language and how to appeal to him indirectly through style and gesture.

Kate is first mentioned in the third sentence of the book, and she is constantly in touch with Binx; as Sharon reports, many people say they are married. Yet Binx's efforts to evade Kate's love and the serious commitment she represents cause him to diminish the importance of her presence for his narrative readers. Thus, the authorial reader must infer much about her importance in Binx's life. For example, from the knowledge she displays of his ideas about movies, it is evident that they have lengthy conversations together that Binx does not report. Just as Binx knows the language of the Catholic catechism well enough to banter with Lonnie about sacrifice and grace, Kate knows about Binx's search and understands his notion of repetitions and rotations. When they attend *Panic in the Streets* together, she asks "'Is this part of the repetition? Part of the search?'" (69)

Because he cannot let himself see the degree of her romantic interest in him and of his attachment to her, Binx has developed strategies for ignoring her or dismissing her advances as signs of her mental instability. Like John Marcher in James' *Beast in the Jungle,* he seeks for something and yet refuses to recognize what is in front of him. Kate says "'[i]t is possible, you know, that you are overlooking something, the most obvious thing of all. And you would not know it if you fell over it'" (70). Not having read his Henry James and thus unable to recognize the parallels between his search and Marcher's wasted life, Binx answers with a dull "'What?'" and then is puzzled: "She will not tell me. Instead, in the streetcar, she becomes gay and affectionate toward me. She locks her arms around my waist and gives me a kiss on the mouth . . ." (70). Still Kate has achieved her purpose, for in spite of his insistence to *his* readers that he loves Sharon Kincaid, Percy's readers note that it is to Kate that Binx's mind repeatedly returns.

There are three scenes in particular in which Percy zooms his lens in upon Kate's romantic overtures to Binx and his unconscious evasions. One of the frequent hints that Kate and her step-mother may actually be scheming to make this match occurs as Binx prepares to speak with Kate for the first time in the action. His aunt has summoned him for the purpose of this meeting, and as he prepares to descend to the basement to speak with Kate, he notes: " . . . I can see my aunt sitting by the fire. . . . She opens her eyes and seeing me, forms a soundless word with her lips." When Kate tells him a few minutes later that she and his aunt talk about him all the time, there is a slight hint that he may be on the verge of suspecting that this whole meeting has been staged, but Kate quickly changes to her "objective" tone which distracts his possible suspicion. Her pose and gestures during this scene, however, are reminiscent of a movie scene played by Bette Davis. As Binx observes, she has even gotten into costume for this tête-à-tête: "As if to emphasize her sallowness and thinness, she has changed into shirt and jeans. She is as frail as a ten year old, except in her thighs" (39). Just as he has shared with her at previous times his search and ideas about moviegoing, perhaps he may also have revealed—as he does throughout the text—the attraction he feels toward certain boyish characteristics in women (he later notices Sharon's boyish cheek and boy's pants) and his weakness for women's hips as their most sexually exciting feature. But her particular costume certainly triggers the appropriate fantasies: he remembers that "Sometimes she speaks of her derrière, sticks it out Beale Street style and gives it a slap and this makes me blush because it is a very good one, marvellously ample and mysterious and nothing to joke about." He says that at the moment "[s]he has the advantage of me . . ." as she taunts him about his mission from his aunt to counsel her. "'You're to tell me all sorts of things,'" she says, but when he falters, she says prophetically: "'It will end with me telling you'" (39-49).

Even as Binx reports small details of her appearance and movements he continues to believe that his interest in her is no more than paternal. "She is in tolerable good spirits. It is not necessary to pay too much attention to her." But pay attention he does, in spite of himself, and perform she does: "Kate stretches out a leg to get her cigarettes. . . . Pushing back her shingled hair, she blows out a plume of gray lung smoke and plucks a grain from her tongue. She reminds me of college girls before the war, how they would sit . . ., seeming old to me and sullen-silent towards men . . ." (41). Could Kate's pose be consciously designed to give him this repetition and take him back across the void of the last ten years after the war to the vitality of his early twenties? The extent of the couple's past intimacy is suggested when Kate's new scientific tone suddenly reminds him of conversations they used to have about her social work, and one case in particular comes to Binx's mind: he remembers Kate saying "'—and all the while it was perfectly obvious that the poor woman had never experienced an orgasm.' 'Is such a thing possible!' I would cry and we would shake our heads in the strong sense of our new camaraderie.'" Given Kate's appeal and the direction of Binx's thinking, it is not surprising that he brings up the matter of her impending marriage to Walter. But now he is coming too close to her anxieties, and she uses his breach as an opportunity to start a quarrel. The terms of the argument, however, suggest what may be on both of their minds. She accuses him and his aunt of patronizing Walter at lunch. But when she uses the phrase "'[w]hat a lovely pair you are,'" referring to Binx and Emily, he turns it to themselves: "'I thought you and I were the pair,'" to which Kate snaps "'You and I are not a pair of any sort.'" Binx remarks to the reader, "I consider this" (41-43).

Given the fact that only a few minutes before Binx felt that it was "not necessary to pay any attention to Kate," this serious act of consideration of this remark represents quite a heightening of interest, yet he seems still oblivious to the possible design for him that may underlie her series of sexual gestures. But designs are certainly being made upon him by his aunt, as he discovers in the next scene when she proposes that he move back to her home and prepare to attend medical school. Both his aunt Emily and his mother have long hoped that Kate and Binx should be married. Does Emily have this in mind for Binx's future, as well, and is Kate's approaching wedding date and her real love for Binx the actual source of her present psychic crisis? But marriage is a word that Binx never uses in regard to Kate, until she proposes it.

On the night that Kate comes to see Binx at three A.M., and he fears for her mental state, he tries to humor her by speculating about how they could live together. He has come into money and speculates about buying a service station and living his life in his present apartment; almost casually he says, "'We could stay on here at Mrs. Schexnaydre's. It is very comfortable. I might even run the station myself. You could come sit with me at night, if you liked.'" To this rather dreary prospect, which would not at all seem to suit Kate's romantic mood of the moment, she still replies with enthusiasm "'You sweet old Binx! Are you asking me to marry you?'" "'Sure,'" he says while telling the reader "I watch her uneasily." Binx expects her to play off of this bantering remark in their usual language games, but to his surprise and dismay, he sees that she is serious. Kate exclaims, "'Not a bad life you say. It would be the best of all possible lives,'" and Binx despairs: "She speaks in a rapture—something like my aunt. My heart sinks. It is too late." Binx's conclusion is that Kate has slipped over the edge emotionally and is no longer herself, but his mental association of the tone of her voice with that of his aunt is most significant, especially in view of the later situation where she and her step-mother live together with him and laugh at his expense. This time Binx recognizes the movie actress that Kate is playing: "—as enraptured and extinguished in her soul, gone, as a character played by Eva Marie Saint," but he fails once more to understand that he is not just a casual observer of her performance but her intended audience (95).

The turning point in their relationship occurs on Sunday night when Kate proposes that she accompany him to Chicago. The preparation for that suggestion is especially well-staged. He is again being sent—this time by Sam—to counsel her. Even Sam appears to further the relationship by depicting Kate as a Russian princess of the old aristocracy and by apparently proposing to her himself, which Kate later reports to Binx to make him jealous. Although Kate is supposed to be in a very disturbed mental state, she seems quite well-prepared for this meeting:

> Kate sits . . . and cheerfully makes room for me in the loveseat. Not until later do I think why it is she looks so well: she is all dressed up for the first time since Christmas. It is the scent of her perfume, her nylon-whispering legs, the white dress against her dark skin, a proper dress fluted and flounced and now gathered by her and folded away from me. (141)

Though Binx remembers this picture later, at the time he is distracted and appears to pay little attention to her. As she talks on, he is listening to the dinner conversation from downstairs. Perhaps detecting his distraction, she picks up upon the idea that he had proposed marriage again: "'I thought about your proposal and it seemed to me that it might be possible after all'" (143). While Binx appears not even to notice this remark, he does begin to become sleepy—the same reaction he had when his aunt told him of her plans for his life and the same reaction he has later on the train. Like Jack Burden in Warren's *All the King's Men*, Binx escapes into sleep. When he awakens, he is on the train with Kate on a kind of pre-marriage mock honeymoon. Binx is still drowsy, and Percy adds a touch of Freudian humor to Binx's dream on the train when Binx imagines standing in line in a crowded bookstore to buy a copy of *Technique in Marriage*: "I noticed that nearly all the crowd jamming against me are women, firm middle-aged one-fifty pounders" (151). If his fear is that women are pressing in on his life and that he may need such a book in his relationship with Kate, it is soon borne out when Kate seduces him and he proves impotent.

In his non-fiction works, Percy often writes about linguistics and the function of language, and he has commented upon the concept of defamiliarization that he learned from the Russian formalists. Binx plays with the notion of defamiliarization when he speaks of how the movies take aspects of ordinary life and make them more real by putting them on the screen. His experience of seeing *Panic in the Streets,* in a theater in the very neighborhood in which the film was shot, defamiliarizes the area for him and enables him to see it more clearly. Similarly, Binx describes his experience of talking with his half-brother Lonnie about religion as decentering language and thus making it better able to be heard: "Lonnie's monotonous speech gives him an advantage, the same advantage foreigners have: his words are not worn out. It is like a code tapped through a wall. Sometimes he asks straight out: do you love me?" (131). By altering the usual form of speaking, Lonnie gets Binx's attention. Lonnie is the only other character besides Kate who also understands Binx's way of reading movies, and the experience of seeing *Fort Dobbs* at the drive-in with Lonnie is for Binx "a good rotation" (116-17).

Less apparent is the skillful way that Kate uses the process of defamiliarization to get Binx to see her more sharply. By altering her speaking style, tone, and gestures and playing out roles from the stage and screen in the character of her own person, she alters and varies her self-presentation. For example, in her telephone conversations with Binx she is unconventional: he says "[f]or some reason or another she feels obliged to keep one jump ahead of the conventional. When I answer the phone, instead of hearing 'Hello, this is Kate' [which Kate knows would be everydayness], there comes into my ear a low-pitched voice saying something like: 'Well, the knives have started flying,'" which he then has to interpret: "which means that she and her mother have been aggressive," or "'What do you know, I'm celebrating the rites of spring after all,' which turns out to mean that she has decided in her ironic and reflected way to attend the annual supper given for former queens of the Neptune Ball." She ends this conversation by hanging up abruptly. Binx observes: "There comes a silence and a click. But this doesn't mean anything. Abrupt hang-ups are part of our analytic way of talking." The only danger with Kate's device is that what is first defamiliarized may soon become conventional. But she strives to keep him off guard (57-58).

There are two key passages that would seem to weigh against the suggestion that Binx is guided toward his fate, consciously or unconsciously, by Kate. One is the exchange in which Kate says that she will only be able to survive in marriage if he tells her what to do. First, appealing to his sense of mission and duty, she says she is "never too bad" when she is with him; then, touching his own insecurity and reversing roles, she says that he is "nuttier" than she is. The point that Binx is really sicker than Kate is made throughout the book, and is, I believe, correct. Next, she reminds him of his marriage proposal and successfully provokes his jealousy by saying that Sam has also proposed. Then, she suddenly shifts her tone to a hard-boiled Brett Ashley style, and she risks all by forcing him to defend the notion that they could make a successful marriage: "'Can't you see that for us it is much too late for such ingenious little schemes?'" Binx notes that her voice is steadier, but he attributes this change to the motion of the train. By this tactic, however, she forces Binx for the first time to take a stand in favor of their marriage, but after they debate the issue, it is clear that Binx still does not take her seriously. As he says, "I do not, to tell the truth, pay too much attention to what she says" (153-55).

But shortly Kate takes a new tack: She "shakes her head in the rapt way she got from her step-mother," and she resorts to complete female submission. She tells Binx he is her God ("'You are the unmoved mover'"), and that the marriage will work if in all things he should tell her what to do. She proclaims her total submission to his will and gives him a passionate kiss. This ancient strategy of declaring her own helplessness serves a double function: it assuages Binx's fear of women by making him feel that she is unthreatening, and it encourages him to think of her as easily seduced. She is, like Alice Doan in *The House of the Seven Gables*, hypnotized by a man's power and open to the suggestion of his will. Meanwhile, lest Percy's readers begin to think that Kate is really not in control of this scene, he has Binx look out the window at a symbol of female power: "The moonlight seems palpable, a dense pure matrix . . ." (156-57).

Binx, however, is not an easily moved, unmoved mover, so Kate takes a more direct approach: "'I feel awful. Let's go to your roomette.'" There she tells him of her discussion with her psychiatrist about her desire to have an affair, and calling Binx "Whipple," she reports her sexual fantasies sparked by reading "a Frenchy version" of *Tillie the Toiler* comics in which Tillie is taken by Whipple in the stockroom. Later when Binx tries to explain his sexual failure with Kate to his imagined Rory Calhoun, he admits: "The truth is I was frightened half to death by her bold (not really bold, nor whorish bold but theorish bold) carrying on." So while on the surface, it may seem that Kate is putting herself in his control, she actually uses shifts in tone and gesture, and antic poses to direct the entire scene; the only thing she cannot control is Binx's libido. The final word goes to Kate, who invokes both Romeo's Juliet and Hamlet's Ophelia in her mocking "'Good night, sweet Whipple. Now you tuck Kate in. Poor Kate. . . . Good night sweet Whipple, good night, good night, good night.'" Percy, of course, invokes Eliot in *The Wasteland* (157-159).

Even if the seduction is a physical failure, however, it is a psychological victory for Kate, for when they arrive in Chicago the next day, Kate assumes firm and permanent command of the relationship. "Kate looks after me," he says (160). Binx has become a submissive husband even before the wedding as Kate attends to the practical details of life, just as she had purchased the train tickets while he slept. The extent of her dominance is most apparent in the scene after his confrontation with Aunt Emily. The meeting itself deserves attention, for Emily is a master of style and gesture, employing the rhetoric of the Puritan jeremiad and the Enlightenment language of republican virtue to chastise him while wielding a sword-like letter opener: "We both gaze down at the letter opener, the soft iron sword she has withdrawn from the grasp of the helmeted figure on the inkstand." In a phallic recollection Binx notes that the tip of the sword was bent because as a boy he had used it to try to pry open a drawer, and he still worries that she suspects him. Hypnotized by her gestures, he cannot take his eyes off the sword: "We watch the sword as she lets if fall over the fulcrum of her forefinger. . . . Then, so suddenly that I almost start, my aunt sheathes the sword and places her hand on the desk. Turning it over, she flexes her fingers and studies the nails. . . ." If Kate has been learning some of her gestures from her stepmother, as Binx earlier suggested, she has a powerful model to imitate (174-76).

When a limp Binx leaves this meeting, he meets a Kate who is "as brisk as a stewardess" flying high as she tells him "'You're stupid stupid stupid. . . . I heard it all, you poor stupid bastard'" (180). She directs him to go home and wait for her, which he dutifully does. But when she does not arrive in fifty minutes, he panics and tries to call Sharon. When her roommate says she is out with her fiancé, he makes a play in Brando style for the roommate. Only when he sees Kate's "stiff little Plymouth"—a car more fitting Binx's puritan nature than his MG—does Binx regain composure. Then, for the first time, he accepts the idea that he will marry Kate by announcing that she is "my own fiancée, Kate Cutrer" (183). In case the symbolism of Emily's sword and the name Cutrer which Kate and Emily share is lost on the reader, Percy earlier had Binx meet a knife salesman who exhibits what Binx refers to as his "cutter." It is significant that Binx did not tell his aunt that he was going to marry Kate, since that would have made all the difference in her attitude toward their trip together to Chicago. Kate rebukes him for the oversight, and again calls him an "idiot." While he wants to attribute his silence to stoic heroism, it is more likely that, as perhaps wary-eyed Kate suspects, he still had not accepted the proposal of marriage as genuine. To seal the matter, Kate immediately tells her aunt herself who is then soon reconciled to him, as Emily should be since he is going to do everything she wished.

The other scene that might suggest that Kate is as weak and dependent in their relationship as she pretends to be is the final one in the Epilogue in which she tells him that she cannot go downtown without knowing that he is thinking about her constantly. This is a curious situation, because he has just explained that within the past year she went on her own on a lark to hear Marian Anderson perform in Dallas—certainly a much bolder trip than a streetcar ride downtown. But close reading of the scene suggests another possible motive for her claim of dependency.

In this relationship dependence is mutual, and Kate knows Binx well enough to understand *his* precarious psychic state. She is always in danger of having him drift away into his dreams of the search, into sleep, or into total psychic withdrawal. Just as she had devised strategies to get his attention before marriage, so she must constantly defamiliarize herself to hold his interest and keep the marriage alive. In this final scene Percy has Kate give a small demonstration of her continued use of cinematic gestures. She has Binx pick a flower with which she then strikes a pose. She tells him to picture her in a very particular way: "'I'm going to sit next to the window on the lake side and put the cape jasmine in my lap. . . . And you'll be thinking of me in just that way?'" (190-91)

By having him think of her in this defamiliarized and highly particular image of her—not a vague image of a wife—she forces herself upon his imagination, just as she had done with her antic poses during their courtship. In the final image of *The Moviegoer*, as an entranced Binx watches her, Kate frames herself as in a scene from a movie: "Twenty feet away she turns around. 'Mr. Klostermann? Mr. Klostermann.' I watch her walk toward St. Charles, cape jasmine held against her cheek, until my brothers and sisters call out behind me" (191).

The reason for the ambiguity of the ending of *The Moviegoer*, then, is that for Binx's narrative audience the ending presents only one side of a more complex situation that Percy has inscribed in the text indirectly for his authorial audience. Binx believes that he has made independent and conscious choices, grounded in his reading of Kierkegaard, to move from the aesthetic to the moral and the religious stage of spiritual development. He believes that he has accepted responsibility to take care of Kate and to embrace all of the values that he had so fiercely rejected earlier, including living in "one of the very shotgun cottages done over by my cousin Nell" (187). But even that term "shotgun," which evokes the image of a man marrying against his will, reminds the authorial reader that Binx's final situation was not exactly his idea. He is like Miles Coverdale in *The Blithedale Romance*, who thought he was in love with the girlish Priscilla but was actually entranced by the more sexually threatening Zenobia. On Friday, Binx thought he was in love with Sharon, but by Wednesday he was engaged to Kate.

As in all novels with unreliable narrators, the authorial reader is privileged to view the narrator's world in a larger frame than he can himself perceive. In that larger world, it is Kate who saves Binx, and in so doing perhaps also saves herself. For Kate and Emily recognize that he is their white hope for any future the Bolling family and the South may have. Binx is a Quentin Compson who lives because Kate holds his attention. By learning his secret language of moviegoing, and using the gestures and techniques of communication of the cinema—such as shifts in tone, cuts, framing, and posing—she makes herself into a character in the movie he wishes his life to be. Playacting as Ophelia, Juliet, Eva Marie Saint, a Russian Natasia, Bette Davis, and Tillie the Toiler, she gives him the experience of the heightened reality, as he calls it, of the movies that he longed for in his life. Just as her aunt has the power to scare the wits out of Binx in a way that he confesses to find "not altogether unpleasant," Kate keeps herself in his mind so that his document, as he calls the book, is on the conscious level an account of his search for the meaning of life amidst modern malaise and everydayness, but is on the unconscious level a record of how people may learn from art how to survive everydayness and create interest and meaning for one another.

Notes

[1] *The Moviegoer* (New York: Knopf, 1961). All references are to this edition.

[2] Of the several existing volumes of interviews with Percy, the most useful for this essay is Lewis A. Lawson and Victor A. Kramer, [eds.] *Conversations with Walker Percy* (Jackson: U Press of Mississippi, 1985).

[3] Of the recent studies of Percy's life and thought, I found the following most helpful: Jerome Taylor, *In Search of Self*: Life, Death and Walker Percy (Cambridge, MA: 1986); essays by Harold Bloom and Tony Tanner in *Walker Percy*, ed. Harold Bloom (New York, 1986); William Rodney Allen, *Walker Percy*: A Southern Wayfarer (Jackson: 1986); Jack Tharpe, *Walker Percy* (Boston, 1983) and the collection he edited, *Walker Percy*: Art and Ethics (Jackson: 1980); Panthea Reid Broughton, *The Art of Walker Percy*: Stratagems for Being (Baton Rouge, 1979); Mary K. Sweeny, *Walker Percy and the Modern World* (Chicago, 1987); Martin Luschei, *The Sovereign Wayfarer*: Walker Percy's Diagnosis of the Malaise (Baton Rouge, 1972); John Edward Hardy, *The Fiction of Walker Percy* (Urbana, 1987); Robert Coles, *Walker Percy*: an American Search (Boston, 1978); Patricia Lewis Poteat, *Walker Percy and the Old Modern Age*: Reflections on Language Argument, and the Telling of Stories (Baton Rouge, 1985).

[4] Lawson and Kramer, *Conversations with Walker Percy* 278.

The Exclusionary Nature of *The Moviegoer*

Timothy K. Nixon

As a student of Søren Kierkegaard and a devout Catholic, Walker Percy displays in his writing the truth of the paradoxical term "Christian existentialism." Percy's protagonists are usually doubting, even morose individuals who search for and approach some insight that will make sense of a senseless world. The protagonists in Percy's novels come to some form of stability after a period of agnostic doubt by making their own "leaps of faith." Thus the seemingly contradictory terms, "Christian" and "existentialism," are reconciled in his writing. Percy's work, therefore, tends to be affirming for those readers who share in the protagonists' doubts and agnosticism. This affirmation leads critics like Linda Whitney Hobson to say in *Understanding Walker Percy*, "In his fiction and his nonfiction Percy attempts to offer a new view of man—man as a 'sovereign wayfarer'—one who has the power to make choices about how he will live and think, thus sovereign. . . ."[1] It is not without import, however, that Hobson uses gender-specific language in this assessment of Walker Percy's writing, for women in his novels are denied the sovereignty which the male protagonists achieve. This sexual specificity appears in his first novel, *The Moviegoer* (1961), as well as in his later fiction, such as *The Second Coming* (1980). Whether Percy made a conscious choice in writing fiction that is male-centered or not, there is an exclusionary nature to his novels. Female characters in Percy's writing are inspirations or hindrances to male characters searching for truth; they are not spiritual questers themselves. One can see, then, that this limitation of female characters' roles can and does limit, or even exclude, female readers from the intended audience of *The Moviegoer*.

Women reading Walker Percy's *The Moviegoer* could possibly find affirmation in their own quests for spiritual enlightenment, if they were not forced to view the female characters as "the other." Binx Bolling's mother represents to him the non-transcendent. Binx's cousin Kate, on the other hand, inspires him with the knowledge necessary to make his leap of faith. But in neither of these cases, nor regarding the other women in *The Moviegoer*, is a female character the seeker. The women are all set in opposition to the male, who searches for enlightenment.

Despite the fact that the protagonist of *The Moviegoer* is a male, women could theoretically read his experience as similar to their own. In their essay "The Reader's Construction of Meaning: Cognitive Research on Gender and Comprehension," Mary Crawford and Roger Chaffin suggest that this ability for women to ally themselves with a male protagonist is due to the fact that women have been conditioned by a predominantly male canon that reflects an androcentric society. Similarly, in her essay "A Map of Rereading: Gender and the Interpretation of Literary Texts" Annette Kolodny utilizes a powerful image to express this same point: "Though masters need not learn the language of their slaves, the reverse is never the case: for survival's sake, oppressed or subdominant groups always study the nuances of meaning and gesture in those who control them."[2] Due to the training in allying themselves with male protagonists that women in American culture receive, it would be possible for them to read *The Moviegoer* and find relevance for themselves in its philosophical encouragement—if they were not constantly reminded of their status as "the other," the position to which all of the female characters in the novel are relegated by their relationships with Binx Bolling, the protagonist.

Identification with the female characters (who serve as inspirations or hindrances to Binx Bolling's enlightenment) inhibits a woman from identifying with the protagonist and denies her the novel's philosophical affirmation. The importance of identification in the act of reading has been explored by several theorists. Laura Tracy utilizes much of Georges Poulet's study of reading in her work "'Catching the Drift': Authority, Gender, and Narrative Strategy in Fiction." Tracy writes that "Poulet predicates the act of understanding the text correctly on an initial act of identification by the reader, who will later exercise his or her critical faculty in order to articulate a textual interpretation."[3] A woman reading *The Moviegoer*, then, would have to identify with Binx Bolling, the protagonist, in order to be part of the philosophical reassurance that the text propounds. Yet allying herself with Binx would force the female reader to place herself in a precarious, uncomfortable relation to the female characters in the novel.

Women reading male texts are required to place themselves as critics of other women in order to identify with a protagonist, which demonstrates the real insidiousness of exclusionary writing. This choice that the female reader must make between the protagonist and her own gender is not asked of male readers. Patrocinio Schweickart decries this subversion of the female reader in her essay "Reading Ourselves: Toward a Feminist Theory of Reading." Schweickart writes, "Androcentric literature is all the more efficient as an instrument of sexual politics because it does not allow the woman reader to seek refuge in her difference. Instead, it draws her into a process that uses her against herself."[4] The female reader of *The Moviegoer* tries to identify with the protagonist Binx Bolling, yet the relationship Binx has with his secretaries, his aunt, his mother, and his cousin Kate consistently works to discourage her from making this identification. By identifying herself with Binx Bolling, the female reading *The Moviegoer* is forced to share his feelings of disdain and near lechery for her own gender and, by extension, herself.

The relationship that Binx Bolling has with his secretaries, which is exemplary of his attitude towards women, is one aspect of the novel *The Moviegoer* that inhibits women from identifying with its protagonist. Objectification best describes Binx's attitude towards his secretaries. Oftentimes his secretaries are nothing more to him than new sexual exploits. Linda Whitney Hobson comments on this sense of woman as conquest in her book *Understanding Walker Percy*. Remarkably, Hobson seems to make no sort of moral judgement of his behavior; she writes,

> Another way to avoid the malaise—the pain of loss—is to experience rotations, "the quest for the new as the new, the reposing of all hope in what may lie around the bend." Nowhere is this seen more concretely in *The Moviegoer* than in Binx's succession of secretaries. When he tires of Linda, he hires Sharon. She is not a "self" to him, but simply an embodiment of "the new."[5]

Hobson's observation that "she is not a 'self' to him" is indicative of Binx's attitude. Binx even admits his tendency to objectify women in his relationship with his secretaries: "Naturally I would like to say that I had made conquests of these splendid girls, my secretaries, *casting them off one after the other like old gloves*, but it would not be strictly true" [emphasis added] (M 8). How much more objectified can a woman be than when she is compared to a glove that is worn and discarded? Furthermore, Binx's wish to admit that he used his secretaries this way cannot "be strictly true" because he feels his time with them was too close to being love affairs. Despite the fact that the relationships had something of a feeling of a love affair for Binx, his attitude towards women remains the same. A female reader could not easily identify with a protagonist who admits to regarding women as mere sexual objects were it not for her being acclimated to this position by the androcentric acculturation discussed by Crawford and Chaffin.

Regardless of her acculturation, a heterosexual woman reading *The Moviegoer* could find identification with Binx problematic because of the physical attraction that Percy emphasizes in Binx's relationships with his secretaries. Though Percy has Binx ogling women throughout the novel—the woman on the bus (M 12-13), Joyce leaning on the windowsill (M 123)—Sharon, the secretary, receives ample attention. Referring to Sharon, Binx thinks, "Her bottom is so beautiful that once as she crossed the room to the cooler I felt my eyes smart with tears of gratitude" (M 65). At another point in the novel, Sharon's body leads Binx to tears when he thinks, "How beautiful she is. She is beautiful and brave and chipper as a sparrow. My throat catches with the sadness of her beauty. Son of a bitch, it is enough to bring tears to your eyes" (M 130). One also notices in this instance that Binx has a proclivity for referring to women as animals, usually birds and horses. Nevertheless, Binx insists that Sharon is beautiful, and this is especially telling when one considers it in light of a comment he makes later in the novel. Fearing that Kate will be deterred by beauty, Binx spurns it by saying, "Beauty is a whore" (M 196). Sharon, his secretary, a beauty—and therefore a whore—could prove a stumbling block to Binx. She becomes, by implication, a whore, and this attitude towards her simply affirms the attitude voiced by Binx himself that women should be worn out and thrown aside. Furthering this objectification of his secretary, Binx says of her, "this fine big sweet piece, Sharon" (M 144). Percy has his protagonist using vulgar language here. Males use the term "piece" to relegate a woman to the status of an artwork and, on another level, to reduce her to her genitals. Both aspects of this term are appropriate with Binx's attitudes towards women as seen in his relationship with his secretaries. He sees Sharon as a beautiful object and as a sexual conquest. Once again, a female reading *The Moviegoer* would more than likely find it difficult, if not impossible, to identify with a character whose attitude towards women was so unflattering.

The relationship that Binx has with his secretaries, moreover, is indicative of his attitude towards all the women in the novel. For instance, at one point in the novel Sharon is juxtaposed with Binx's own mother. This juxtaposition confirms the assumption that he has a disregard for all women, not just his secretaries. After taking Sharon to his family's camp, Binx makes a comparison of his mother's and his secretary's voices. He thinks to himself,

> the talk of the women, easy in its silences, come together, not in their likenesses (for how different they are: Sharon's studied upcountry exclamations . . . and my mother's steady catarrhal hum . . .) but come together rather in their womanness and under the easy dispensation of the kitchen (M 161).

Seemingly innocuous, this comment upon the voices of the two women and their place—in the kitchen—adds a new, similarly derogatory, dimension to Binx's attitude towards women.

Binx acknowledges that the women are in some aspects dissimilar ("not in their likenesses"), yet when together in their place of domesticity, they are alike to him. These women are forced to deal with the mundane; they must prepare the meals for the group at the fishing camp. While Binx is relaxing on the porch, he compares the two women, in his leisure-time, lofty thoughts, because of their being caught in the menial. This meniality is what Binx despises in his mother. Upon his arrival at the fish camp, Binx thinks about his mother: "After a while her domesticity will begin to get on my nerves. By the surest of instincts she steers clear of all that is exceptional or 'stimulating.' Any event or idea which does not fall within the household regimen, she stamps at once with her own brand of the familiar" (M 138). Has it occurred to Binx that his mother is cooking and cleaning for six children—one severely handicapped—her husband, herself, Binx and his guest, as well as working as a nurse? She would not have much time or energy left for lofty, transcendent thoughts.

Just as Binx assumes he knows the motives of his mother's actions, Claude Richard in his essay "The Exile of Binx Bolling: Walker Percy's *Moviegoer*" assumes that Binx's mother exists in the mundane and menial because she likes it. Richard writes,

> The mother is apprehended in the serene activities of her preparing meals, in her dedication to the commonplace. . . . The ordinary is her only passion. But its practice is not simple; it is a choice . . . based on a marvelous instinct . . ., a constant discipline of insertion into the everyday.[6]

Richard's choice of the term "serene activities" as referring to the care of a large family is ludicrous. He seems to be making some idyllic experience out of clothing, feeding, and cleaning up after six children and a spouse. Likewise, Richard refers to Binx's mother's meniality as a "passion," a "choice," an "instinct," and something which requires "constant discipline." These phrases are not synonymous and, therefore, demonstrate the illogic of Richard's claim. Binx is a first-person narrator with limited knowledge of the psyches of the other characters, and Richard seems to have assumed Binx's credibility. What is interesting, however, is Richard's unknowingly calling attention to Percy's use of the patriarchal dichotomy: woman as physical and immediate and man as spiritual and transcendent.

Whether or not, however, Binx's mother exists in the mundane out of choice or a lack thereof, she functions as an antithesis to the spirituality of her son. As in Binx's comparison of the two women in the kitchen and in Richard's summation of Binx's mother being stuck "in the everyday," women are assigned a position in the temporal. This lack of transcendence is the plague crippling Percy's protagonist. Linda Whitney Hobson views Percy's struggle in these exact terms. Hobson writes, "Percy's Catholicism affirms the importance of transcending 'everydayness,' a term for the malaise besetting postmodern or post-1945 man which Percy took from philosopher Gabriel Marcel."[7] The novelist, therefore, and the protagonist appear to be in opposition to the female, whom they see as stuck in the non-transcendent. A woman would only be able to find spiritual affirmation in identifying herself with a misogynist, if she were to disregard her sex and do it in spite of the misogyny.

Binx's mother is not the only female obstacle to his spiritual enlightenment; Binx's Aunt Emily is a deterrent to her nephew's leap of faith. Claude Richard sees Aunt Emily as Binx's one "true adversary, the only system of thought capable of obstructing his becoming."[8] Linda Whitney Hobson identifies Aunt Emily with those forces which lead Binx astray from his path to enlightenment; she writes, "His [Binx's] father's family, represented by Aunt Emily, pulls him in the direction of stoicism."[9] And similarly, William Rodney Allen writes in his book *Walker Percy: A Southern Wayfarer* that "Aunt Emily's 'soldierly' response to life represents for Binx a forgetting a evasion [sic] of his search."[10] All three of these critics of the novel, therefore, view the character of Aunt Emily in an antagonistic light. Aunt Emily is seen as a force trying to dissuade Binx from overcoming his despair, trying to prevent the protagonist from coming to fulfillment. To identify with this protagonist who has overcome the temptation, as it were, of the female would prove highly problematic for women reading *The Moviegoer*.

To attempt identification with the female characters would be difficult, too. The character of Aunt Emily, for instance, does not readily allow identification for female readers, on account of her sexual ambiguity. Allen uses the term "soldierly" in the above quotation to describe Aunt Emily, and later in his book he likens her to "Plato's philosopher/kings."[11] Binx himself uses male imagery to describe his aunt; he thinks, "With her blue-white hair and keen face and terrible gray eyes she is somehow at sixty-five still the young prince" (M 27). However, the most significant example of Aunt Emily's mixed gender is where she herself takes on the role of the male relative in speaking with Binx:

> I did my best for you, son. I gave you all I had. *More than anything I wanted to pass on to you the one heritage of the men of our family*, a certain quality of spirit, a gaiety, a sense of duty, a nobility worn lightly, a sweetness, *a gentleness with women*—the only good things the South ever had and the only things that really matter in this life [emphasis added] (M 224).

The legacy Aunt Emily hopes to pass on to Binx in the above quotation sounds suspiciously like the sentiments a father would give to his son, even regarding the way he should treat women. Percy's treatment of Aunt Emily here parallels Hemingway's characterization of Pilar in *For Whom the Bell Tolls*. In both instances the female character who demonstrates intelligence and assertiveness loses her womanhood; she is, as Judith Fetterley says in *The Resisting Reader: A Feminist Approach to American Fiction*, "immasculated." Therefore, a female reader, finding it difficult to identify with Binx Bolling because of his misogyny, must come to terms with the treatment of the character of Aunt Emily. A woman reading *The Moviegoer* and not finding it possible to identify with the character of Binx could begin to identify with one of the female characters, such as Aunt Emily; in so doing, though, she is endangered of being aligned with the unsexed or immasculated.

Kate is another problematic female character. Not only is she emotionally unstable—and perhaps due to that fact—Kate vacillates between curtness and coyness, manipulation and incompetence. Her purpose in the novel, it seems, is to serve as a foil. When Kate needs direction, Binx is there to give it. She is the passive to his active. Binx searches for God. Kate searches for someone (some man) to tell her what to do. She, in her helplessness, is also the impetus for Binx's enlightenment. Most critics agree that

Percy denies Kate any significance of her own; she is important primarily for her relation to Binx. Anne Goodwyn Jones addresses this aspect of Percy's *The Moviegoer* in her study *Tomorrow Is Another Day: The Woman Writer in the South*. Jones comments on Kate's place in the novel:

> Kate depends on Binx not just for guidance and money; her very existence itself is a function of his imagination, of his thinking of her "just that way." Wary of self-expression, invented and sustained by Binx, she acts for him as well. . . . her traditional role permits his. For as a southern gentleman, Binx may now make decisions, take responsibility, be gentle but authoritative. At the end of the novel, then, both are climbing into the shell of southern tradition in the hope of surviving the middle of the twentieth century.[12]

As Jones suggests here, Kate serves as a catalyst for Binx's enlightenment, whereas his mother and aunt are hindrances to it.

Linda Whitney Hobson concurs with Anne Goodwyn Jones's analysis of Kate's significance in the novel. Hobson feels that Binx "chooses the intersubjective relationship . . . of standing transparently before Kate and then before God."[13] Echoing this interpretation, Mary K. Sweeny states in her book *Walker Percy and the Postmodern World*, "When Kate finally arrives 'sooty-eyed and nowhere,' he [Binx] is able to hope. . . . He is able to slowly surmount his despair."[14] Like so many deified female images in this culture, Kate has become the path upon which the male climbs to his transcendence. There is an echoed suggestion of the inspiring wife in the scene of Binx's visit to his friend in Chicago. Binx deifies the wife of his friend Harold; she "is beautiful in just the same way: blond hair waving down her cheeks like a madonna, heavenly blue eyes, but stooped so that her should-blades flare out in back like wings" (M 209). Kate as Binx's wife-to-be, then, parallels Harold's wife, the ideal of motherhood and domesticity which even leads the husband toward the ethereal. Thus, this characterization allows little possibility of a female reader's identifying with Binx, since the reader would be a member of the inspiring sex, not the inspired.

Anne Goodwyn Jones does not fault Percy for this limitation of Kate. She views the function of Kate in *The Moviegoer* as indicative of society, especially in the South. Jones accuses Binx's—and Percy's—society for relegating Kate to the position of inspiration when she writes, "It is sad and ironic that the very traditions whose uncomfortable acceptance permits Binx and Kate to escape the anonymity of what Binx calls 'scientific humanism' should deprive Kate of the chance to seek identity and autonomy while offering

Binx that very opportunity."[15] Regardless of the fault, whether society's or Percy's, Kate is not a figure capable of her own transcendence; she is merely a tool to be utilized in the enlightenment of a male protagonist.

Ironically, Kate's inspiring Binx comes about because of her vulnerability and passivity. Finding someone more despairing than himself seems to be what leads Binx to his salvation. On their trip to Chicago, Kate plants the seed of Binx's salvation through valor when she tells him, "What I want is to believe in someone completely and then do what he wants me to do" (M 197). Kate appears to be frightened of or at least unwilling to accept the responsibility for her actions; she is searching for a dependable figure who is not paralyzed by this same fear. Binx's struggle for enlightenment culminates in Kate's realization that he is her dependable figure. She says, "I am frightened when I am alone and I am frightened when I am with people. The only time I'm not frightened is when I'm with you" (M 234). Her dependence upon him assures Binx that his earlier proposal of marriage to Kate was the appropriate thing, for taking care of her will provide him with a path to his own transcendence.

This chivalric attitude leads to Binx's enlightenment because it provides him with the validation his life does not otherwise have; just as Binx feels that watching a movie in the neighborhood where it was filmed validates the neighborhood, becoming a dependable protector and guide for someone else validates his existence. As Mary Sweeny suggests, Binx "has an intense awareness of life, which he shares with Kate, whom he hopes to snatch from the pit of her despair,"[16] thereby providing a purpose for his own life. Likewise, Claude Richard claims in "The Exile of Binx Bolling" that Binx must provide Kate with those things she lacks: stability, health of mind, order, balance, seriousness, liberation, a center.[17] Binx, then, has discovered his purpose when he claims, "There is only one thing I can do: listen to people, see how they stick themselves into the world, hand them along a ways in their dark journey and be handed along, . ." (M 233). Binx must help Kate, someone less certain of things than himself. Again, in his own words Binx sets up the opposition between himself and Kate: he helps others, and she is helped.

The search, the quest that Binx Bolling has led since his being wounded in Korea, concludes when he decides to protect and shelter his depressed cousin Kate. Binx sees that there are others who suffer, if not more, in different ways than he. Binx must be strong for Kate, who is crippled by her gender, just as he must be a strong figure for his handicapped half-brother Lonnie. The enlightenment Binx experiences is an acknowledgement of his duty to other people. There is no apparent reconciliation of his agnosticism. The piety of the man coming from the Ash Wednesday service sparks Binx's epiphany, while Kate, sitting in the car next to him, continues to be uninspired. Binx is reassured by coming to some spiritual truth that compassion for other seeking individuals is all that he can do. Kate, on the other hand, is reassured by knowing that she will soon marry Binx and have someone to tell her what he wants her to do. The only development Kate experiences is selflessness, giving in to total passivity. Conversely, Binx's enlightenment is active; he must help people "along a ways in their dark journey."

This difference in the spiritual development of Binx and his cousin Kate is indicative of the way female characters are treated throughout the novel. Those stereotypes of women (women as Eve or Virgin, for instance) that have become cliched run throughout *The Moviegoer*. Kate is an inspiration for Binx along his path to spiritual enlightenment. She is at other times the purpose of his enlightenment, when she needs protecting. Woman, in this instance, is relegated to something between Beatrice and the Virgin Mary. Juxtaposed to Kate's role as inspiration, Binx's mother becomes ironically a temptation. Binx dislikes his mother for her meniality. By being stuck in the everyday, she dissuades her son from transcending. Likewise, Aunt Emily encourages Binx to accept a philosophy foreign to him, also tempting him to forfeit his spiritual quest. Woman, in this instance, is relegated to an Eve character. She is the temptress; she tempts the protagonist to forget his spiritual essence. Women in *The Moviegoer* also act as temptations to Binx in a purely sexual context. Female characters are shallow sex objects, for example Binx's secretaries. Moreover, some female characters in the novel are unsexed on account of their aggressiveness or intelligence, such as Aunt Emily. In any case, women in *The Moviegoer* are stereotypes denied development. Binx Bolling, the male protagonist, on the other hand, strives for and reaches a new level of stability in his beliefs.

The realization that Binx comes to in order to make his leap of faith and attain spiritual insight is reaffirming for those individuals like Binx who do not settle for agnosticism alone but try to find an answer to their questions. Identification with the protagonist Binx might enable readers to make their own "leaps of faith," encouraged by the optimism of Percy's writing. Nevertheless, identification with Binx is highly problematic for female readers, and the encouragement offered to readers of Percy's novel *The Moviegoer* is denied them. Women reading *The Moviegoer*, should they try to identify with the protagonist, will find themselves in a precarious position, being forced to define themselves against members of their own gender, or being forced to realize the futility of their search, for the female is a tool for male enlightenment. Moreover, the female is forced to sacrifice her gender, as Aunt Emily did, if she subscribes to an androcentric philosophy. Furthermore, Binx's objectification of his secretaries is an aspect of the novel that should set most female readers in opposition to him initially, thus thwarting their ability to identify themselves with him. As seen earlier, a woman does have the ability to identify with a male protagonist, so a female reading *The Moviegoer* could possibly identify herself with Binx, if it were not for the fact that, as Patrocinio Schweickart says, in so doing "she confirms her position as other."[18]

Notes

[1] Linda Whitney Hobson, *Understanding Walker Percy* (Columbia: U of South Carolina P, 1988) 24.

[2] Annette Kolodny, "A Map of Rereading: Gender and the Interpretation of Literary Texts," *The Critical Tradition: Classic Texts and Contemporary Trends*, ed. David H. Richter (New York: St. Martin's Press, 1989) 1136-note.

[3] Laura Tracy, *"Catching the Drift": Authority, Gender, and Narrative Strategy in Fiction* (New Brunswick: Rutgers UP, 1988) 6.

[4] Patrocinio P. Schweikart, "Reading Ourselves: Toward a Feminist Theory of Reading," *Gender and Reading: Essays on Readers, Texts, and Contexts*, ed. Elizabeth A. Flynn and Patrocinio P. Schweikart (Baltimore: Johns Hopkins UP, 1986) 42.

[5] Hobson 33.

[6] Claude Richard, "The Exile of Binx Bolling: Walker Percy's *Moviegoer*," *Critical Angles: European Views of Contemporary American Literature*, ed. Marc Chenetier (Carbondale: Southern Illinois UP, 1986) 88.

[7] Hobson 13.

[8] Richard 91.

[9] Hobson 38.

[10] William Rodney Allen, *Walker Percy: A Southern Wayfarer*, (Jackson: UP of Mississippi, 1986) 28.

[11] Allen 26.

[12] Anne Goodwyn Jones, *Tomorrow Is Another Day: The Woman Writer in the South, 1859-1936* (Baton Rouge: Louisiana State UP, 1981) 7.

[13] Hobson 41

[14] Mary K. Sweeny, *Walker Percy and the Postmodern World* (Chicago: Loyola UP, 1987) 58.

[15] Jones 8.

[16] Sweeny 31.

[17] Richard 103.

[18] Schweickart 50.

Keeping Quentin Compson Alive:
The Last Gentleman, The Second Coming, and the Problems of Masculinity

Susan V. Donaldson

William Faulkner's Quentin Compson always held a special fascination for Walker Percy. "He's sick of time," Percy told Jo Gulledge in a 1984 interview, "because time means the past and history. So he tears the hands off his watch. He's wandering and wanders around this godforsaken Boston suburb, and the last place he wants to go is back to Mississippi, to time and history" (Con 299-300). By and large Percy tended to associate his own protagonists, like Binx Bolling in *The Moviegoer* and Lancelot Andrewes Lamar in *Lancelot*, with a similar desire to flee history and he saw himself as "starting where Faulkner left off, of starting with the Quentin Compson who *didn't* commit suicide." As he remarked in the Gulledge interview, "Suicide is easy. Keeping Quentin Compson alive is something else. In a way, Binx Bolling is Quentin Compson who didn't commit suicide" (Con 300).

But if Quentin Compson exemplifies for Percy the contemporary southerner in flight *from* tradition, Faulkner's most famous character also serves as a highly appropriate symbol *of* tradition—of white southern masculinity under siege—for both Faulkner and Percy. In an increasingly hostile and alien world, Quentin represents the traditional white male aristocrat whose sense of honor is betrayed by time, change, and most tellingly, by women and black subordinates to whom his status is undeniably linked. Significantly, suicide emerges as the only recourse through which Quentin can finally assert what remains of male honor as defined by his family and his region. That same sense of besieged male honor also defines the shadowy dead father who looms over Percy's two novels about Williston Bibb Barrett—*The Last Gentleman*, published in 1966, and *The Second Coming*, issued in 1980. In a manner of speaking, Will Barrett's father, whose suicide drives both narratives and nearly destroys Will's life, is Quentin Compson redux, and if Will Barrett himself is to come to terms with that suicide, he must also confront the peculiarly destructive version of masculinity and tradition that his father represents. Such a confrontation, though, offers its own peculiar dangers, in particular the possibility of reaffirming as well as questioning regional traditions and their peculiar notions of manhood.

Percy himself, in fact, would probably be the first to admit that his character Will Barrett, *The Last Gentleman*, and *The Second Coming* have strong ties to the past and tradition—a tradition, moreover, deeply rooted in the South's obsession with honor, violence, and gender boundaries. From the very beginning of *The Last Gentleman*, we are told that Will Barrett's dreamy and anonymous life in New York City "was part of a family pattern." As the narrator notes, "it was an honorable and violent family, but gradually the violence had been deflected and turned inward." A forthright man of action, Will's great-grandfather "knew what was what and said so and acted accordingly and did not care what anyone thought" (LG 9). Packing a pistol in the streets of his small Mississippi town, he even once challenged the Grand Wizard of the Ku Klux Klan to an impromptu shoot-out. A generation later, Will's grandfather "seemed to know what was what but he was not really so sure," being one who "gave much thought to the business of being brave" (LG 9-10). Equally brave is Will's own father, but for him most of all even mere existence "was a strain." Ultimately, " . . . he was killed by his own irony and sadness and by the strain of living out an ordinary day in a perfect dance of honor." No wonder, then, that Will Barrett himself, "the last of the line," simply "did not know what to think" and hence had resorted to becoming "a watcher and a listener and a wanderer" (LG 10).

If anything, Will finds his family tradition and its definition of masculinity to be something of a burden, and his frequent bouts of amnesia represent nothing so much as the desire to free himself from the chains of the past and from the demands of southern manhood. As the narrator notes, "It was the olden time with its sweetness and its great occasions which struck a dread to his heart" (LG 258). In this respect, of course, he has a good deal in common with Quentin Compson in *The Sound and the Fury* and *Absalom, Absalom!*. For Quentin, like Will, also yearns periodically for escape from the garrulous ghosts of the past who seem to tell the same stories over and over again.

But if Quentin yearns for escape, he also feels duty-bound to abide by the code of honor that he has inherited and that defines him as a white southern gentleman. That code of honor in particular requires a fierce allegiance to family and a determination to defend the moral reputation of one's womenfolk, whose moral standing symbolizes that very sense of honor. As Quentin himself muses at one point in *The Sound and the Fury*, " . . . Father and I protect women from one another from themselves our women. . . ." In defense of that honor, Quentin rashly throws himself into two fights for which he is ill equipped. Significantly, he opens both fights with a single, ritualistic question—"*Did you ever have a sister*?"[1]

Quentin's opening question suggests something of the formalized and gender-bound nature of such violent encounters. It is, I would argue, just this sort of ritualized violence that links Quentin Compson and the Barretts in *The Last Gentleman* and *The Second Coming* to the tradition of white southern manhood in general. For violence and aggression appear to have been an inextricable part of masculinity in a region where gender differences, as historians like Steven Stowe have suggested, were probably more extreme and pronounced than they were elsewhere in an era notable for its rigid demarcations between masculinity and femininity[2]

In particular, Bertram Wyatt-Brown observes in *Southern Honor*, being an elite white man in the nineteenth-century South meant asserting aggressive behavior and authority at an early age, knowing one's place in the midst of an elaborate hierarchy of inferiors and superiors, venerating one's father, defending one's family and taking violent revenge for offenses, and guarding the reputation of one's mother, sister, wife, and daughter. Being a man of honor also meant loving and fearing women, with whose moral uprightness and standing in the community male honor was intimately bound. Noting the violence of response to epithets like "son of a bitch," Wyatt-Brown declares: "The intensity of feeling arose from the social fact that a male's moral bearing resided not in him alone, but also in his women's standing. To attack his wife, mother, or sister was to assault the man himself."[3]

That male honor, authority, and identity were paradoxically dependent on an intricate web of relationships with subordinates accounts in part, both Stowe and Wyatt-Brown argue, for the repressed tensions with which the southern family and the community of white upper-class men reverberated.[4] The mere *appearance* of that authority was all too susceptible to subversion by inferiors, whether by women or by blacks, precisely because the behavior and reputation of subordinates helped define the very nature of elite white male identity.[5] Hence in this decidedly problematic world the duel or affair of honor often served as the principal means for resolving questions and tensions—at least temporarily. For the duel stood, in Kenneth S. Greenberg's words, "at the core of antebellum white male culture" by serving as a ritualistic assertion of masculinity, a ceremony largely determining who did indeed belong to the closed circle of white upper-class men.[6] Indeed, to participate in a duel was to assert one's membership in an elite community of white men, and that membership in turn insured the white male's authority over subordinates.[7]

Asserting this sort of traditional manhood, though, is far more complicated for Quentin Compson in *The Sound and the Fury* and *Absalom, Absalom!* and Will Barrett in *The Last Gentleman* and *The Second Coming*. For both Quentin and Will confront what appears to be an unfamiliar and even hostile world, one resistant to the very notion of male honor. Indeed, in the rapidly changing landscape of the twentieth century traditional modes of masculinity could no longer be taken for granted. By 1900, as historians Peter Filene and Joe Dubbert have argued, men "were finding it acutely difficult to 'be a man'." Filene in particular observes: "The concept of manliness was suffering strain in all its dimensions—in work and success, in familial patriarchy, and in the dimensions that Victorian Americans did not often discuss aloud, sexuality." A good deal of that strain, of course, had to do with changing roles of women and the rise of feminism. The prospect of female equality boded ill for nineteenth-century cultural constructions of masculinity because men, in Filene's words, "depended on women to mark the ambivalences in their definition of manliness. The patriarchal economy of sex was disintegrating because 'the better half' seemed willing to be only equally good."[8]

But perhaps nowhere did change in the "patriarchal economy of sex" hold more portent that in the early twentieth-century South. The very foundation of white southern masculinity—an elaborate hierarchy of authority and deference intertwined with rigid definitions of race, class, and gender—seemed to be in danger of disintegrating in the face of socio-economic change. Increasing political activism among blacks and women suggested that traditionally defined subordinates could no longer be counted upon to help define the boundaries of white male identity. Moreover, in the economically straitened years of the late nineteenth and early twentieth century, white men found it increasingly difficult to perceive themselves as protectors, providers, and patriarchs. The resulting gender and racial tensions, Joel Williamson has argued persuasively, helped formulate the mythology of black rapists seeking out white women and exploded all too often in lynchings serving as ritualistic reenactments of white male authority over blacks.[9]

Such tensions no doubt also contributed to a heightened uncertainty about masculinity characterizing southern writers like William Faulkner and Walker Percy. In this respect, of course, Faulkner and Percy had a good deal in common with a host of other twentieth-century male writers for whom, in Virginia Woolf's words, "virility [had] now become self-conscious."[10] As Peter Schwenger has noted, twentieth-century male writers often found themselves pondering the notion of masculinity from a self-conscious perspective antithetical to the more traditional notion of male authority as "natural" and inherent. Self-conscious musings tended to weigh intellect against physicality, thought against action, hesitation against self-assurance. Above all, those musings threatened to expose gender definitions as cultural, artificial constructions rather than as "natural" and unchanging modes of being.[11]

It is, I would argue, precisely this sort of self-consciousness and hesitation about white southern masculinity that marks both Quentin Compson in *The Sound and the Fury* and *Absalom, Absalom!* and Will Barrett in *The Last Gentleman* and *The Second Coming*. Over and over again both characters implicitly contrast their own sense of masculinity with more traditional forms. Repeatedly, both characters find themselves to be less than "men" in the sense inherited from family and regional tradition. Their uncertainty about their masculinity is perhaps most pronounced in their relationships with those subordinates who have traditionally defined the boundaries of white southern manhood—blacks and women.

Stranded in early twentieth-century Massachusetts, Quentin in *The Sound and the Fury* recognizes with a sudden sharp prescience that black subordination to white authority is merely an elaborately constructed fiction: "That was when I realised that a nigger is not a person so much as a form of behaviour; a sort of obverse reflection of the white people he lives among." Equally problematic are Quentin's relations and perceptions with women, whose very unpredictability threatens the way Quentin and his father define themselves as men. Thinking back on talks with his father, Quentin muses: " . . . *They have an affinity for evil for supplying whatever the evil lacks in itself for drawing it about them instinctively as you do bedclothing in slumber fertilising the mind for it until the evil has served its purpose whether it ever existed or no. . . .*"[12] Underlying those meditative passages on the female affinity for evil is the unspoken assumption that women of the present generation—in particular Quentin's sister Caddie—have failed the white men with whom their fates are inextricably linked. For Quentin and his father Caddie is both lady and whore, sister/daughter and fallen woman, and her easy transgression of proscribed gender and sexual boundaries exposes the shaky foundations of the Compson men's sense of masculinity.

So potent is the threat offered by the unpredictable behavior of "inferiors" like white women and blacks that there simply seems to be no room any longer for the sort of white male honor by which Quentin and his father define themselves. What remains is the lingering sense of defeat that permeates Quentin's section in *The Sound and the Fury* as well as a finely tuned ironic vision. As Quentin thinks, " . . . *Father said it used to be a gentleman was known by his books; nowadays he is known by the ones he has not returned. . . .*"[13]

It is that element of irony—as well as its potential for comedy—that draws Walker Percy's eye in *The Last Gentleman*, which, like *The Sound and the Fury*, explores the plight of a southern gentleman lost in a confusing modern world. "Oh, to be like Rooney Lee," Will Barrett thinks longingly from time to time (LG 265). For like Henry Adams, who describes Robert E. Lee's son in half-contemptuous and half-envious terms in *The Education of Henry Adams*, Will is both attracted and repulsed by the sort of quintessentially white southern masculinity—its physicality and gift for command—that Rooney Lee seems to embody. Will, of course, is singularly lacking in those traits, and he tends to identify them with his family's lost tradition of heroism, honor, and violence, the tradition that he finds himself unable to emulate.

What Will lacks in particular, though, is that elaborate web of deference and subordination that made Rooney Lee's flair for masculine command and self-assurance possible in the first place. Like Quentin, in fact, Will can never quite be certain where he stands with either blacks or women. Indeed, so attuned by his own personal radar is Will to everyone who surrounds him that he is utterly unsure who or what he himself is. Unlike traditional white southerners, the narrator tells us, Will looks directly at the blacks around him and does so with unease, compassion, and incomprehension. Partly because of that unease he never quite knows where he ends and they begin. Exquisitely attuned to the vulnerability of one young black man in particular, Will thinks unexpectedly, "I should have been born a Negro, for then my upsidedownness would be right side up and I'd beat them and life would be simple" (LG 198). At least then, the narrative implies, he could have made some sense of his apartness and disorientation: he would have known who and what he is.

Most slippery and confounding of all, though, are Will's relationships with women—in particular, with Kitty Vaught, the young southern girl he half-heartedly courts throughout the narrative. For one thing, Will never quite knows where he stands with Kitty, in part because her own sexuality appears to him elusive and problematic. On more than one occasion, we're told that "she was like a boy turned into a girl" (LG 177). For another, Kitty by Will's lights seems to be far too much at home in a world of modernity and change. Her very character seems to change with her environment—urban and bohemian under her sister-in-law Rita Vaught's tutelage and cheerfully collegiate among her Alabama sorority sisters. Exasperated with this mercurial quality, Will wishes that " . . . she would chew Juicy Fruit like a proper Alabama girl" (LG 106) and frowns upon her casual use of terms like "psychosexual": "She was his sweetheart and ought to know better. None of your smart-ass Fifty-seventh Street talk, he felt like telling her" (LG 73).

Will finds Kitty especially disorienting because he has learned from his embittered and gentlemanly father lessons about women all too similar to those taught by Mr. Compson to Quentin Compson in both *The Sound and the Fury* and *Absalom, Absalom!*. "Go to whores if you have to," his father once tells him, "but always remember the difference. Don't treat a lady like a whore or a whore like a lady" (LG 100). To know the difference, the elder Barrett implies, is to be a gentleman, even in an age he denounces as one of fornication. But the problem is that Will does indeed have difficulty telling the difference because the women around him elude the categories of virgin and whore he had inherited from his family's gentlemanly code. With a jolt of surprise he finds himself "pressing against girls, rassling around in elevators and automobiles" (LG 88), and Kitty herself occasionally demonstrates that she is far less concerned about her "virtue" than he is. And the more unpredictably the women around him behave, the more confused Will becomes about himself: "But what am I, he wondered: neither Christian nor pagan nor proper lusty gentleman, for I've never really got the straight of this lady-and-whore business. And that is all

I want and it does not seem too much to ask for once and all to get the straight of it" (LG 180).

But in the world that both Will Barrett and his father inhabit—as well as the world in which Quentin Compson lives—the only way to "get the straight of it" appears through suicide—through an internalized affair of honor requiring self-destruction. Like nineteenth-century duels, suicide ultimately emerges as the only recourse for the traditional white southern male to retain his honor. Only through self-destruction, apparently, can he resolve his problematic relationships with women and black subordinates and questions about his own masculinity. Only through a duel with himself, so to speak, can he answer once and for all the questions raised over and over about his manhood. Only through death can he finally assert his membership in the closed community of white male aristocrats.

When Mr. Compson in *The Sound and the Fury*, for instance, tells Quentin, " . . . we must just stay awake and see evil done for a little while its not always . . .," Quentin replies, " . . . it doesn't have to be even that long for a man of courage. . . ." Suicide, Quentin hints, is the last gesture of manhood in a world that no longer acknowledges male honor, a final assertion of elite masculinity. Not incidentally, suicide also provides Quentin with escape from a world of ambiguities into the timeless, insular realm of death, where his sister Caddie can be protected, traditional masculinity and femininity restored, and honor reclaimed. "*If it could just be a hell beyond that*," he thinks, "*the clean flame the two of us more than dead. Then you will have only me then only me then the two of us amid the pointing and the horror beyond the clean flame. . . .*"[14]

It is this recourse—this final affair of honor—that lies submerged beneath the comedy and picaresque adventures of Will Barrett in *The Last Gentleman*. For the single most important and elusive incident in the narrative is the suicide of Will's father, the one memory that Will himself can never quite confront until the end, the memory that explains his difficulty in recalling the past. Weaving in and out of the narrative, the elder Barrett's suicide is the only means, the novel suggests, by which that distant figure can finally claim his standing in a closed circle of elite white men that in actuality no longer exists. Killing himself, ultimately, becomes the only weapon he can use to assert his sense of authority over those he considers his inferiors. Of his enemies, Will Barrett's father says, "Once they were the fornicators and the bribers and the takers of bribes and we were not and that was why they hated us. Now we are like them, so why should they stay? They know they don't have to kill me" (LG 330). But he adds to his son, "They may have won, but I don't have to choose that," and when Will asks "Choose what?" he answers quite simply, "Choose them" (LG 330-31). It is just a few minutes after that exchange that Will hears the sound of the gunshot, the sound that resonates throughout both *The Last Gentleman* and *The Second Coming*.

It is this choice, finally, that faces both Will Barrett and his friend Sutter Vaught in *The Last Gentleman*. For strangely enough, Sutter Vaught, the unregenerate rake who is the scandal of his family, thinks in much the same terms as the elder Barrett, that is to say, in rigid either/or terms. Either he commits suicide, he muses in his journal, or else he allies himself wholeheartedly with "lewdness," the "sole concrete metaphysic of layman in age of science=sacrament of the dispossessed" (LG 279), and with "pornography in order to set it at naught" (LG 281). Tellingly, Sutter is himself strongly drawn to the alternative of suicide as the last act of the man of integrity, and it is he who articulates the range of choices facing Will Barrett, who like his father before him contemplates the prospect of self-destruction:

> Which is the best course for a man: to live like a Swede, vote for the candidate of your choice, be a good fellow, healthy and generous, do a bit of science as if the world made sense, enjoy a beer and a good piece (not a bad life!). Or: to live as a Christian among Christians in Alabama? Or to die like an honest man?" (LG 379).

The ending of *The Last Gentleman* seems to imply that both Sutter and Will finally reject suicide as the one last assertion of unequivocal manhood. Will, for one, now seems able to reject the either/or choices pondered by Sutter as too extreme, and Sutter himself, who has hinted periodically of his own plans for suicide and who actually seems to be carrying out those plans in the last few pages, stops and waits when Will frantically hails him. On the face of things, then, the choice represented by the elder Barrett, as well as his particular mode of masculinity, *seems* to be repudiated by Will in the end.

But those last few pages have an odd, ambiguous air to them, as though both Sutter and Will have finally confronted not the choice itself but the *necessity* of making a choice. The very last line, which notes merely that Sutter "waited" for Will, suggests anticipation far more so than closure, the *beginning* of resolution rather than the resolution itself (LG 409). That sense of anticipation in turn indicates that Will Barrett has a good deal of unfinished business to face—business with his father, with the choice of suicide, with southern honor, and with southern manhood.

Above all, Will Barrett and Walker Percy himself face the unfinished business of keeping Quentin Compson alive, and it is that prospect that shapes the narrative of the sequel to *The Last Gentleman*, titled with equal measures of profanity and reverence *The Second Coming*. Published in 1980, *The Second Coming* focuses on a prosperous and middle-aged Will Barrett twenty-five years after the events of *The Last Gentleman*. And though the second novel titillates its readers with satirical comments on southern tourism, evangelicalism, secularism, retirement anxieties, and suburban anxieties, the primary concern of *The Second Coming*, I would argue, is with the self-destructive masculinity represented by both Will Barrett's father and Quentin Compson. Indeed, the second novel returns to the problem of traditional white southern manhood and its links to suicide with a frequency bordering on the obsessive. What emerges is not just a narrative that lays bare the terrifying events half-repressed and half-revealed by the narrative of *The Last Gentleman* but a dialogue articulated from the perspectives of two different notions of manhood—one deeply rooted in the tensions and ambiguities of white male southern honor and one that has yet to define itself in counterpoint.

By and large, though, that dialogue is remarkably one-sided precisely because both Will and Percy himself appear to find that traditional notion of manhood so compelling. From the very beginning of *The Second Coming* Will Barrett struggles earnestly to keep from following Quentin toward self-destruction, but the power of the past appears to be as strong for Will as it is for Quentin. In the opening chapters Will is hurled almost immediately back into the past, first to high school days and then to the day forty years ago in a Georgia swamp when his father tried to shoot both his son and himself. Having shuttled aside that searing memory for decades, Will finds himself throughout the novel repeatedly reenacting the very gestures he made on that day—gripping a shotgun, stepping over a barbed wire fence, and peering for quarry and his father. So palpable is the presence of the past in Will's present that everything is marked by "a certain mocking sameness" (SC 51). Nothing, Will thinks, has changed since that day; nothing has really happened to him except that one event. Even Will and his father "*are the same*," as the father's ghostly presence repeatedly asserts (SC 55).

Indeed, however different Will's life in a North Carolina resort community may be from that of his father's in Mississippi, Will is still marked by his father's legacy of southern manhood, figured, significantly enough, in the four possessions from his father's house that Will still owns: copies of *Ivanhoe* and *Lord Jim*, a Luger pistol, and a Greener shotgun. No other possessions could symbolize as effectively that curious combination of chivalry and violence, honor and self-destruction, physical derring-do and introspection, which Will sees as his patrimony. Tellingly, the only way that Will can interrupt his own "spells" of melancholia and find a fleeting moment of authentic selfhood is to fire the Luger as close to his face as possible. Only then, the narrator notes, is it "possible to see oneself briefly as a man among men rather than a self sucking everything into itself . . ." (SC 14). Only then, brushing with death, can Will briefly find himself and his "manhood."

In this respect, of course, he has all too much in common with his father and with Quentin Compson, both of whom can assert male honor only through violence and self-destruction. For like Quentin in particular, Will's relationships with those traditionally designated as subordinates are problematic at best and his own status as a traditional white southern man is far from certain. Yamaiuchi, Will's Asian servant, and Ewell McBee, a local poor white turned video entrepreneur, indicate singularly little interest in showing Will traditional deference. Yamaiuchi periodically ignores Will's orders, and McBee tells Will quite frankly, "The only difference between you and me is money. Outside of that, you and I are exactly alike" (SC 177). Nor can Will count on deference from the women in his life to bolster his sense of traditional manhood. From his born-again daughter to Kitty Vaught Huger, long married and now a brassy lady golfer, the women around him turn out to be unpredictable and even a little threatening at times. Even Will's dead wife continues to exert a formidable presence. It is, after all, her money and social position that have bestowed wealth and power upon Will himself.

No wonder, then, that Will periodically explodes with rage, the sort of rage that also characterizes two other besieged white southern men—his father and Quentin Compson. As the unrelenting presence of the elder Barrett tells him, "*You're one of us*" (SC 171). Suicide, the final affair of honor, will be Will's end too, or so the apparition of Will's father would seem to insist.

Yet Will also yearns desperately to escape that sense of besieged manhood, and his yearning accounts for the furious quarrel in which he engages with his ghostly father throughout the novel.

All Will has ever wanted since that day in Georgia, he tells his father, was to get "out from you and from the Mississippi twilight, and from the shotguns thundering in musty attics and racketing through funk-smelling Georgia swamps, . ." (SC 72). Above all, Will longs for another definition of manhood altogether, one that does not require violence and self-destruction for its ultimate validation. To his father's apparition he declares:

> And I was never so glad of anything as I was to get away from your doom and your death-dealing and your great honor and great hunts and great hates (Jesus, you could not even walk down the street on Monday morning without either wanting to kill somebody or swear a blood oath of allegiance with somebody else), yes your great allegiance swearing and your old stories of great deeds which not even you had done but had just heard about, and under it all the death-dealing which nearly killed me and did you. (SC 72)

But merely to make this assertion is not enough. So powerful is the presence of the past, of old notions of manhood, of Quentin Compson's narrative of self-destruction, that Will is locked in a life-or-death struggle with his father's ghostly presence throughout the whole of the novel. That struggle suggests nothing so much as a time-honored affair of honor. The duel even begins in traditional fashion—with an ever-increasing spiral of insults questioning each other's masculinity and authority.[15] Facing down his father, Will savagely equates the elder Barrett's last act of self-destruction with auto-eroticism:

> And what samurai self-love of death, let alone the little death of everyday fuck-you love, can match the double Winchester come of taking oneself into oneself, the cold-steel extension of oneself into mouth, yes, for you, for me, for us, the logical and ultimate act of fuck-you love fuck-off world. . . . (SC 148)

At this point, though, the duel culminates not in a final showdown with his father but, oddly enough, with God himself. For it is after that last venomous insult that Will lands on his plan to force God into acknowledging His existence and Will's. "What I am doing," Will observes, "is asking God with the utmost respect to break his silence. No, not asking. Requiring" (SC 192). Only by challenging God, apparently, can Will Barrett assert his own sense of self and authority, make sense of the baffling world around him, and restore to himself some sort of order and reassuring manhood.

But there is something strangely unpersuasive about this section of the novel, much like the ending of *The Last Gentleman*. It is as though Will is merely postponing the inevitable—the ultimate showdown with his father and with his own suicidal impulses. For one thing, Will is far too easily distracted from that metaphysical duel with God—first by a toothache, then by his abrupt exit from the cave into an abandoned greenhouse, and finally by an unexpected romance with, of all people, the daughter of his old sweetheart Kitty Vaught Huger, Allie Huger. For another, the narrator takes considerable care to dismiss Will's quixotic challenge as sheer lunacy.

Not until Will's own sense of manhood and authority is directly challenged—this time by his daughter and the local minister, who summarily pack him off to the local nursing home—does Will once again take up the gauntlet and face his ghostly father in a final confrontation. Therein lies the real focus of the narrative. This is the duel, I would argue, that really concerns Percy and engages his energies, not Will's comical sojourn in the cave waiting for God's sign.

This confrontation, moreover, finally brings to the surface the self-destructiveness that Percy sees defining the Barrett family tradition and that is only hinted at in *The Last Gentleman*. Again and again Will finds himself drawn to the Luger and the Greener that represent his father's legacy, and once he even finds himself on a bus bound for Georgia and a reenactment of that fatal day in the swamp. Ultimately, the duel between father and son crowds out the present and Will's romance with Allie Huger, as Will finds himself listening to his ghostly father, who asserts that manhood can be achieved only through the ultimate act of self-destruction. "At least you can do that," the apparition declares, "not only not lose, but win, with one last splendid gesture defeat the whole foul feckless world" (SC 337). Only suicide, his father asserts, can maintain Will's membership in the closed elite circle of men with honor: "Go like a man, for Christ's sake, a Roman, here's your sword" (SC 337).

In this final confrontation Will says no to his father's demand for death and resolutely throws away both the Luger and the Greener. It would appear, then, that Will does indeed succeed in keeping Quentin Compson alive after a prolonged and considerable struggle. But it is significant, I think, that Percy's version of Quentin stays alive largely in terms of the past. He proves his mettle, so to speak, by picking up the gauntlet and finally facing down his father. He participates, in short, in a ritualized form of combat that resembles nothing so much as a traditional southern duel, and he emerges victorious, a man who has proven his worth according to tradition.

Will also emerges, not incidentally, with a new sense of authority, one that hearkens back to a striking degree to nineteenth-century notions of white southern manhood and its elaborate hierarchy of race, class, and gender. Those figures who challenge his authority early on, from Yamaiuchi and Ewell McBee to Kitty Vaught Huger, have miraculously disappeared by the end of the novel. In their place can be found, oddly enough, a newly emerging community of nursing home inmates restored to social usefulness by none other than Will himself. Will's sudden vision of low-cost housing and jobs for the elderly brings this community into being, and implicitly, Will will continue to serve the community as leader, the chief to whom those nursing home inmates owe fidelity and service.

Finally, conquering his father's ghost allows Will to devote himself wholeheartedly to his romance with Allie Huger, whose story of escape from a local mental hospital alternates with the narrative of Will's troubles. Allie's stay in the hospital has left her with a faulty memory and a mode of speech so idiosyncratic that it nearly constitutes a private language. But Will tells her, "I fall down from time to time and you are very good at hoisting. It would be pleasant to have you around to give me a hand." In return, he adds: "I'll be your memory. Then too, your language is somewhat unusual. But I understand it. In fact, it means more than other people's. Thus, I could both remember for you and interpret for you" (SC 329).

By Percy's lights, this relationship and his portrayal of Allie represent a significant development in his fiction. In a 1980 interview, Percy observed: "Women sometimes have charged me with not knowing anything about women, which may be true, but I like what I have done with Allie. I think she is my most successful woman character" (Con 188). Both Allie and Will, he argued, "achieve their lives in a way no other characters I've written about have" (Con 183). And in many respects, Will and Allie together, along with the narrative strategy of alternating their stories, do indeed appear to evoke the ideal of intersubjectivity and mutuality Percy inherited from Martin Buber and celebrated in his theoretical writings on communication.[16]

But that double narrative disappears after Allie and Will's romance begins in earnest. What remains is largely Will's story—his confrontation with his ghostly father and his quest for a new sense of authority and manhood. And the romance with Allie, idyllic as it is, resembles nothing so much as Quentin Compson's searing vision of life after death with Caddie, where male honor and authority are finally restored: "*Then you will have only me then only me then the two of us amid the pointing and the horror beyond the clean flame . . .*" (144). Will, after all, is the one who will do the remembering and the interpreting, and it is Will who takes charge of the direction their lives are to take. Ultimately, his romance with Allie suggests not so much a new ideal of mutuality and intersubjectivity as it does a restoration of authority, honor, and, yes, manhood in a form that Quentin Compson himself would find all too familiar.

Will Barrett's vision of a new world and of new men and women, in the end, is also all too familiar. The dialogue between old and new notions of manhood ends, like Quentin Compson's story, with a monologue, one that sounds all too much like Quentin Compson himself. For if Quentin longs to escape the past and tradition, he yearns for restoration with equal force, and it is that latter yearning—unacknowledged but unmistakably *there*—that permeates the ending of *The Second Coming* to a startling degree. Will Barrett, Percy's New Man, the Quentin Compson who refuses to commit suicide, can never quite bring himself to give up the Quentin Compson who did indeed kill himself. To the end Will holds on tenaciously to that elusive sense of authority and honor, that hierarchical ideal of southern manhood, that very nearly drove him to self-destruction. Keeping Quentin Compson alive, apparently, is not so different from letting him die.

Notes

[1] William Faulkner, *The Sound and the Fury*, corrected text (New York: Random-Vintage, 1984) 110 and 105.

[2] Steven M. Stowe, *Intimacy and Power in the Old South: Ritual in the Lives of the Planters* (Baltimore: Johns Hopkins UP, 1987) xvii.

[3] Bertram Wyatt-Brown, *Southern Honor: Ethics and Behavior in the Old South* (New York: Oxford UP, 1982) 154, 157, 158, 197, 34, and 53.

[4] Wyatt-Brown 174.

[5] Wyatt-Brown 53-54.

[6] Kenneth S. Greenberg, "The Nose, the Lie, and the Duel in the Antebellum South," *American Historical Review* 95 (1990): 62.

[7] Stowe 47.

[8] Peter Gabriel Filene, *Him/Her/Self: Sex Roles in Modern America* (New

York: Harcourt Brace Jovanovich, 1975) 77 and 104. See also Joe L. Dubbert, *A Man's Place: Masculinity in Transition* (Englewood Cliffs, NJ: Prentice-Hall, 1979) 11.

[9] Joel Williamson, *The Crucible of Race: Black-White Relations in the American South since Emancipation* (New York: Oxford UP, 1984) 115-16.

[10] Virginia Woolf, *A Room of One's Own* (New York: Harcourt Brace Jovanovich, 1957) 101.

[11] Peter Schwenger, *Phallic Critiques: Masculinity and Twentieth-Century Literature* (London: Routledge & Kegan Paul, 1984) 9.

[12] Faulkner 98 and 110.

[13] Faulkner 92.

[14] Faulkner 202 and 103.

[15] See Stowe 47.

[16] Elzbieta H. Oleksy, "From Silence and Madness to the Exchange that Multiplies: Walker Percy and the Woman Question," a paper delivered at the Southern American Studies Association Conference, Williamsburg, Virginia, February, 1991 (see pp. 123-133).

"The Cave . . . the Fence":
A Lacanian Reading of Walker Percy's *The Second Coming*

Doreen Fowler

As *The Second Coming* concludes, Will Barrett, who has always felt distanced from his own life, renounces death in all its forms and resolves to seize his life. He has arrived at a formula for living which requires two people—Allison and Father Weatherbee: "Am I crazy to want both, her and Him? No, not want, must have. And will have."[1] But Will can't have both Allison and Father Weatherbee, for to choose one is to rule out the other. Allison, a mother-figure, represents the plenitude of the imaginary with no difference and no absence; Father Weatherbee represents the Law of the Father, the phallus, the signifier of separation and loss. If Will chooses Father Weatherbee, he becomes a speaking subject always alienated in the 'Other';[2] if he chooses Allison, he experiences no lacks of any kind, but ceases to exist as a speaking subject, for the subject is lack. As Percy's novel demonstrates, Will's answer is no solution but yet another formulation of his yearning to resolve the contradiction which is inherent in the constitution of the subject.

Will's problem, as he accurately diagnoses it, is that he "is of two minds," and he envies a hawk darting overhead because the "hawk was not of two minds" (48). Unlike Will, the hawk, repressing nothing, is not split. But Will is a speaking subject, and for him there is a distance between signified and signifier. As a speaking subject, Will has repressed a fused existence in the world, and this repression has opened up the unconscious with his repressed yearning for a lost wholeness.

The split which Will perceives in himself can perhaps be best understood in terms of Lacan's account of the origin of the subject.[3] According to Lacan, at first all children are engaged in an imaginary dyadic relation with the mother in which they find themselves whole. During this period, as Terry Eagleton explains, "no gap has as yet opened up between signifier and signified, subject and world,"[4] and the child lacks any defined center of self. For the child to acquire language, to enter the realm of the symbolic, the child must become aware of difference, for, as Saussure explains, a sign has meaning only because of its difference from other signs.[5] Identity comes about only as a result of difference, only by exclusion. The appearance of the father establishes sexual difference, signified by the phallus, a key-term in Lacanian theory. The entry of the father drives the desire for original unity with the maternal body underground, opening up the unconscious and creating the subject as lack. For this reason, then, Lacan can say the subject is that which it is not, or, as Toril Moi explains, clarifying Lacan, "The speaking subject that says 'I am' is in fact saying 'I am he (she) who has lost something' and the loss suffered is the imaginary identity with the mother and the world."[6]

In *The Second Coming* the entry into the symbolic order is represented during a hunting trip which took place when Will was twelve. In the novel's present, Will, a man in his forties, relives the primordial moment when the subject was split from the world as he passes through a fence which was "a sign of another fence he had climbed through" (51). The fence which Will crosses is "the out-of-bounds fence" (50), on the other side of which he will find Allison, his double, the representative of his repressed self, which he abjured at the age of twelve when he ducked under a fence in a Georgia swamp.

The fence in the "wet cold funk-smelling pin-oak swamp" (54) symbolizes difference, and, as he recalls passing under this boundary, Will realizes that this was "the only event" that "had ever happened to him in his life" (52). With this crossing, he enters the symbolic order, repressing the literal in favor of a symbol. To enter the symbolic is to state the privilege of the phallus, the signifier of loss, over the signified, and so "[e]verything he saw became a sign of something else." The substance is absent, the symbol dominates: "The tiger? Whatever he was, he was gone. Even the wheeling blackbirds signified not themselves but a certain mocking sameness" (51). According to Lacan, "the subject disappears under the being of the signifier."[7] In other words, in patriarchal culture, the symbolic order so dominates the signified that the subject disappears, lacks being. Lacan even uses the word, 'castration,' for the relation of subject to signified. Paraphrasing Lacan, Jane Gallop explains that paradoxically a man assumes the attributes of his sex—becomes a man—only through a threat, the threat of castration.[8] The domination of the signifier, the phallus, over the signified requires the son to repress—cut off—a part of the self, the body's experience.

Accordingly, Will's entry into the Law of the Father is a symbolic castration and death, for as he crosses the fence his father strips from him his gun:

> He had gone through the fence, but before he could stand up, the man had grabbed his shoulder from the other side of the fence in a grip that surprised him not so much for the pain as for the suddenness and violence and with the other hand grabbed the gun up and away from him, swung him around and cursed him. (52)

Entering the realm of the law, language, and culture which is based on absence and desire, he experiences the assertion of the father's authority and, under the threat of castration, is forced to reject a fused existence with the world and the mother. He is castrated, then, by not being total: "Without his gun," the boy feels "naked and disarmed" (52). That this entry into the civilized order is a rejection of the authentic for a sign is ritually enacted by Will's father's attempt to commit suicide and kill his son. The body's death is the ultimate subordination of authentic existence to the rule of the signifier. Furthermore, as a result of his father's attempt to kill him, Will is deaf in one ear, and this loss of sensation is the outward sign that Will is initiated into the symbolic, an order characterized by difference and distance.

The signified that Will renounces in the swamp is identified with women, particularly with mother-figures, who recall a time before the opening up of difference and the unconscious. For example, one avatar of his own repressed fused existence in the world is Ethel Rosenblum. Will recalls Ethel occupying a space that emblemizes a collapse of difference: "this non-place, this surveyor's interstice. Here's the place for us, the only place not Jew or Gentile, not black or white, not public or private" (8). This "weedy stretch" represents a return to the imaginary, a fusion of conscious and unconscious. Similarly, Ethel herself, as Will pictures her, seems to possess the power to eliminate difference; he recalls Ethel standing at the blackboard factoring equations: "No matter how ungainly the equation, ugly and unbalanced, clotted with complexes, radicals, fractions, *zip zip* under Ethel Rosenblum's quick sure hand they factored out and cancelled and came down to unity, symmetry, beauty" (7). Will desires Ethel, then, as the objectification of his own repressed authentic being. But the acknowledgement of the unconscious, in the words of Jane Gallop, "threatens representation, threatens to return the subject to the powerlessness, intensity and anxiety of an immediate, unmediated connection with the body of the mother."[9] For this reason, Will's desire for Ethel causes him to fall "down into the Johnson grass and the goldenrod, onto the earth smelling of creosote and rabbit tobacco" (8). His fall signals impotence, for to heal the split subject is to collapse the distinctions which constitute the self.

Allie, like Ethel Rosenblum, represents Will's repressed self, which he renounced at his father's command when he ducked under a fence in a Georgia swamp. Will finds Allie when, while golfing, he crosses "the out-of-bounds fence," which recalls to him his boyhood hunting experience with his father. In other words, as Will crosses the fence to find Allie, he is violating the Law of the Father to maintain difference and returning to the maternal body. Allie, like Ethel, represents a loss of distinctions. When Will first sees her, for example, he mistakes her for a boy, then calls her a "youth-girl" (75). Moreover, she seems to represent both a daughter-figure and a mother-figure. Allison, according to Kitty, Allison's mother, might be Will's daughter and seeming to sense a relatedness, Allison repeatedly asks Will if he is her father. But Allison, the all of which he is son, also represents his mother. Repeatedly, she mothers Will, wrapping herself around him, warming him with her stove, reminding him that he is a body in the world. Both the mother who conceives the daughter and the daughter who becomes mother, Allison embodies the relatedness to the other, which Will buried in his unconscious when he was twelve. And now that repressed self returns in the form of Allison, his double, who is "as familiar to Will as he himself" (77).

Allie, then, represents the plenitude of the imaginary, and she refuses to take her place in the symbolic order. For example, while in the Valleyhead sanitarium, she will not speak or participate in group, i.e., she refuses to be a speaking subject. For this repudiation of the Law of the Father, a father-figure, Dr. Duk exacts a symbolic castration—electro-shock therapy. Even after her escape from Valleyhead, language—the hallmark of the symbolic order—is foreign to her, since words are substitutes for absent referents and, for Allie, there is no difference or distance between the signifier and the signified: "She took words seriously to mean more or less what they said, but other people seemed to use words as signals in another code they had agreed upon" (34).[10] Allison's allegiance to the imaginary also explains her mental state. She is borderline psychotic, and Toril Moi writes that "to remain in the Imaginary is equivalent to becoming psychotic and incapable of living in human society."[11] With Allison, then, Percy embodies the imaginary, the original identity and presence.

Time and time again in *The Second Coming* Will Barrett senses that "something is missing" (273), and his search for the missing part always leads him to Allison. For example, the novel's central action, Will's cave-wait, is a search for an absent center; he enters the cave determined to wait there until he has answers to the questions: "*Where is it? What is missing? Where did it go? I won't have it. I won't have it*" (273). Ostensibly Will is searching for God, but the form his search takes suggests that the object of his quest is the absent signified, a return to an original unity with the maternal body and the world; for his search leads him to straddle "the out-of-bounds fence," symbolizing the violation of the Law of the Father, to crawl down into a cave "like a baby getting through a pelvis" (209), and to experience the presence of the material world: "The mountain pressed on his back" (209). Perched in the cave, "quite comfortabl[y] sitting against the curving wall" (211), with water dripping down the side of the chamber, Will resembles the fetus in the womb of the mother.

Significantly, what Will finds as a result of his cave-wait are two representations of his repressed material existence—the tiger and Allison. The tiger Will envisions, with its snout-like muzzle, the same word Will uses to describe his own nose, is a self-portrait. As Will observes, his tiger is nothing like Blake's fierce predatory beast, but rather, given the way it appears to be alternately giving birth, dying, or molting, seems to emblemize the transformative powers of nature. Looking for the missing center, Will has found the body's experience.

Will's search for answers ends when he is delivered from the womb-like cave into Allison's greenhouse. He falls into the greenhouse slippery and headfirst like a baby being born, and Allison cares for him like an infant, feeding him, washing him, carrying him, even removing his feces. In other words, Will has found the absent signified, the fused relationship with the mother and the world which he repressed when he entered the symbolic order. But now, returned to the imaginary, he is helpless, infantalized. He cannot sit up or feed himself. He is dependent on Allison to pour water down his throat to keep him alive. His leg is hurt symbolizing impotence. In sum, Will has reestablished the original dyadic unity and no longer experiences lack, but because the subject is constituted of lack, Will ceases to exist as a subject.

Much as Will longs to heal the split subject, he yearns equally to establish the boundaries which constitute the subject. Thus when Allison returns to her greenhouse after a short absence, she finds Will fallen on the ground: "his one-eyed profile gazed not at her but at the wet cold earth inches away. The eyes bulged in the terrific concentration of pushing the earth away" (255). Even in his helplessness, he is intent on "pushing the earth away," that is, on repressing the literal in favor of a sign.

This, then, is Will's dilemma. With Allison, he finds what is missing and experiences a lost unity and presence, but from this plenitude he always draws back because law, language, and culture are created by exclusion. For example, lying naked together, Will is revitalized by Allison: "her warm body curled around his lard-cold muscle straps and bones, spoon-nesting him, her knees coming up behind him until he was shivering less and, signaling a turn, he nestled her, encircled her as if he were her cold dead planet and she his sun's warmth" (255-56). But from this full and direct access to reality, he retreats—"But he stopped her . . ." (257)—announcing he has to leave, and when he returns minutes later, he is changed, a split subject: "He was different. They stood, the candle between them. She didn't want to look at him" (265). The candle between them symbolizes the phallus, a sign that divides the self from the imaginary, the empty marker of difference. Resisting reabsorption back into the mother and the world, Will re-enters the symbolic order and redefines the nature of their relationship in terms that are compatible with that order. He will be Allison's "legal guardian": "That will involve a fiduciary relationship which I will discharge faithfully, in your interest and to the best of my ability" (265). In other words, he will play the role of a representative of patriarchal law. In response, Allison asks, "Is that all?" And Will answers, "Isn't that enough?" (266). While Allison longs for all, Will will settle for a part, a sign to represent an absence.

Leaving Allison and repressing his desire for unity with the maternal body, Will once again is a divided subject. Not surprisingly, then, as he drives, he experiences double vision: "He saw two roads instead of one, and thinking himself to be on the interstate, took the passing lane, until he saw headlights coming straight at him" (292). After driving off the road, he walks along the highway until he comes to a bus-station restaurant, where he has breakfast and is rather mysteriously joined by a tall man, an avatar of the symbolic order, who embodies the lack of substance at the core of the empty signifier: "Though the tall man stood reared back, feet apart, as if he had a big belly, he did not. Actually he was thin and seemed infirm. . . . His cheeks were pale and withered but his lips curved richly as if they belonged to a hearty man" (293). Even the name that Will uses for the man, the Associate—suggesting the man's participation in a communal order—marks him as a representative of the symbolic order. Also the Associate's life's work, the loan business, corresponds to the way the symbolic operates: the loan business, like the symbolic order, seeks to supply a substitute to cover over and defer loss.

The Associate talks to Will of Georgia "and the word came to him like a sign" (295) because it was in Georgia that Will entered the realm of representation. Given this sign, Will decides to return to the Thomasville swamp, and explains to the Associate that he is travelling to Georgia "to buy in," a phrase that reflects his intention to ritually reenact yet again the primal repression of the signified:

> All these years he had thought he was in luck that it didn't happen and that he had escaped with his life and a triumphant life at that. But it was something else he had escaped with, not his life. His life—or was it his death?—he had left behind in the Thomasville swamp, where it still waited for him. With a kind of sweet certainty he knew now that it was there that he would find it. Finding the post oak—he knew he could walk straight to it—and not coming out at all was better than thrashing around these pretty mountains, playing in Scotch foursomes, crawling into caves, calling on God, Jews, and tigers. (296-97)

Will's thoughts reveal that he emerged from the swamp in Georgia so many years ago with "not his life," that is, having denied authentic existence. And what waits for him there now is a form of castration and death—the cutting off of the body's experience. The post oak which he means to find emblemizes the phallus, with its unreasonable and disproportionate rule over the signified; and his desire to find this post oak figures his yearning to embrace this rule and thus to reject both the material world—the "pretty mountains"—and fusion with the maternal body, to which Will symbolically alludes when he recalls "crawling into caves."

But again Will vacillates. Even as he determines to embrace the empty signifier, he longs for the absent center:

> . . . his eye traveled along the ridge and came to a notch where in the darkness of the pine and spruce there grew a single gold poplar which caught the sun like a yellow-haired girl coming out of a dark forest. Once again his heart was flooded with sweetness but a sweetness of a different sort, a sharp sweet urgency, a need to act, to

> run and catch. He was losing something. Something of his as solid and heavy and sweet as a pot of honey in his lap was being taken away. "I'm not going back to Georgia," he said, rising. (297)

Having resolved to establish difference from the mother and the world in order to create identity, Will immediately experiences the loss of the signified, and once again he switches course. He decides to get off the Georgia-bound bus and return to Allison. But to choose to unite with Allison, the externalization of his own repressed being-in-the-world, is to choose to return to the dyadic unity of the imaginary, a state which Percy dramatizes for a second time in *The Second Coming*.

Returning to Allison, Will re-experiences the same fate which he suffered before when he elected to return to the mother and the world by crawling into the womb-like cave in search of his missing center. From that cave he fell unconscious into Allison's greenhouse and awoke to find himself on her potting table, utterly helpless, and totally dependent on Allison. Now he falls from the bus and is "delivered" (300) by the bus driver to the Linwood Hospital. Once again, he rouses from unconsciousness to find himself stretched out on a table, helpless, his body manipulated by a woman, the female technician. On this occasion, Will wakes to find himself strapped to a moving table. Eventually the table "stood on end like a mummy case" and he "saw stars" (299). Helplessly bound to moving matter, his position aptly concretizes the state of being a body in the universe. This reassimilation into the world-body is also represented by two x-rays, Will's and a woman's, in a "shadowbox": "Next to it a pelvis connected legbones to backbone as simply and comically as a Halloween skeleton. Next, a bigger woman-size pelvis had something new cradled in its womb, a puddle of white. What was hatching here?" (301). The two paired x-rays figure Will and his double, his shadow-self; and his double is imaged here as a fetus in the womb of the mother, the state to which Will returns if he seeks to recover a lost plenitude.

The lesson, then, that Percy's novel reiterates is that the reassimilation of the signified, like its repression, incurs a form of castration. Choosing to return to Allison, a representation of the repressed other, Will once again relinquishes autonomy and is helplessly dependent on a mother-figure. This time he is admitted as a patient in his dead wife's nursing home where his wife's money "took care of everything" (309) and where he is "regulated" (301) and "controlled" (303). The fate of those who elect to re-experience the imaginary identity with the maternal body and the world is objectified clearly in the condition of the men in the nursing home. Mr. Arnold, for example, cannot speak; according to Freud, the inability to speak is an analogue for castration. But Mr. Arnold speaks quite well when he enters into a struggle for control with his roommate. In other words, the assertion of dominance and difference, typical of the patriarchal order, permits Mr. Arnold to become a speaking subject. Castration is even more strikingly evoked in the plight of Mr. Arnold's roommate, Mr. Ryan. One of Mr. Ryan's legs is amputated at the hip, and the other is freshly amputated and bandaged below the knee. Mr. Ryan jokes, "They going to keep chopping on me until I'll fit on a skateboard." Showing Will his stump, he asks plaintively, "Ain't that a pistol?" (317). His word, 'pistol,' a metaphor for the penis, suggests an analogy between his diminished legs and the phallus, the sign of difference. In effect, Mr. Ryan's loss of one leg and the erosion of the other externalizes a gradual process of the loss of difference.

Even as *The Second Coming* concludes, Will continues to vacillate between the symbolic order and the imaginary, between a reassimilation of authentic existence which is a loss of difference, and the assertion of difference based on the exclusion of the literal in favor of an empty sign. Leaving the nursing home, he returns to Allie and resolves to begin his life with her, choosing to re-establish a fused relationship with the mother and the world. No sooner has he made this decision, however, than his contrary impulse asserts itself. Lying in bed beside Allison in a Holiday Inn room, he hears his father's voice commanding him to abjure the world and the flesh, which, according to his father, are "impregnated with death" (337).

Directed by his father's voice, Will rises and walks to a fence in a corner of the Holiday Inn property: "The corner was empty, no pool, no lounges, no tables, no cars, no children's playground. Yet the grass was well trimmed up to the fence separating it from the pasture. He wondered how many people had set foot in this empty corner over the years. Perhaps none" (336). The fence to which Will's father summons him recalls yet again the fence in the Georgia swamp under which Will ducked as his father cursed him and took from him his gun. Like that other fence, this one, which separates the pasture from the well trimmed grass, objectifies the practice of the symbolic order: it excludes the natural world and, by means of this exclusion, difference and meaning are established. Because the Law of the Father demands separation from the maternal body and the world, Will's father commands him to go to a fenced-off place "where nobody's been" (337), and clearly Will's father intends Will not merely to deny the body's experience by relegating it to the unconscious, but at last to separate wholly and irreversibly from the world and the body by taking his own life.

Instead Will pursues the opposite course. He walks to the overlook and hurls into the gorge the Greener and the Luger. He then returns to his room and consummates his sexual relationship with Allison, an act which, with its suggestion of incest, constitutes a reintegration with the mother and the world, prohibited under threat of castration by the Law of the Father.

But even as Will makes love to Allison, still his resolve to heal the split subject is doubtful; for, in describing his lovemaking with Allison, he echoes a key phrase invoked by his father to summon Will to interdiction and death. His father's phrase is doubly significant: it forms the novel's title and it enunciates the novel's central paradox—that the reintegration with the signified, no less than its banishment, is a form of castration and death:

> Come, it's the only way, the one quick sure exit of grace and violence and beauty. Come, believe me, it's the ultimate come, not the first come which we all grew up dreaming about and which is never what we hoped, is it, but near enough to know there is something better, isn't it, the second, last and ultimate come to end all comes. (336-37)

Will's father puns on two meanings for the word, 'come': to experience orgasm; and to die. The use of one word to suggest two meanings has the effect of identifying them, suggesting that, because fusion with the maternal body and the world obliterates the boundaries which constitute the subject, sex is death. Thus later when Will echoes his father's usage of the word, 'come,' to evoke his sexual relationship with Allison—"Entering her was like turning a corner and coming home" (339)—this echo seems to affirm his father's identification of sexual merging with death even as Will is at last satisfying his need to merge with Allison, the representation of his own fused existence in the world.

The novel concludes with Will's final decision; he chooses both Allison and Father Weatherbee: "Am I crazy to want both, her and Him? No, not want, must have. And will have" (360). This decision is no resolution to his conflict, but a restatement of it. Throughout the novel, Will has yearned for two mutually exclusive epistemic registers. He longs to heal the split subject, i.e., to reexperience the lost unity and presence of the imaginary, even as he longs to take his place in the symbolic order, and thus to become a subject separate from the other. In stating his desire for both Allison and Father Weatherbee, Will is merely reiterating his yearning to reconcile irreconcilable opposites: the symbolic and the imaginary.

Clearly Allison, both a mother-figure and a daughter-figure, is a reminder of a fused existence with the world, a representative of the imaginary. Father Weatherbee, on the other hand, is an avatar of a symbolic order that is characterized by separation and distance. For example, Father has devoted his life to putting as much distance as possible between himself and others: he has spent fifty years in a tiny, remote village in the Philippines, and Will finds him secluded in an attic room "strictly off limits to the ladies" (310), where he is operating a toy train. According to Jack Curl, "Father here believes in two things in the world. One is the Seaboard Air Line Railroad and the other is Apostolic Succession" (311). Both of Father's obsessions suggest his unqualified commitment to a patriarchal order that eschews relatedness. The railroad is a symbol of escape and freedom from an engulfing material world. The Apostolic Succession, a ritual passing on of priestly power from one generation to the next by a "laying on of hands," accurately reflects the son's initiation into the male symbolic order; for the son becomes a speaking subject by a form of "laying on of hands"—in Will's case, by his father roughly seizing him and taking from him his gun as he crossed the fence—in other words, by a violent act that symbolizes interdiction and separation.

In sum, *The Second Coming*, like all of Percy's novels, examines the central problem inherent in the formation of the subject. To become a subject is to separate from a fused existence and to experience loss. No sooner does Will reenact his accession into the symbolic order with its attendant splitting than he longs for the absent center, banished to create meaning. But when Will then seeks to reincorporate this lost part of the self that has been split through the creation of identity, he experiences the dissolution of the "I" and reverts to his former position: he hastens to establish the boundaries of the self by once again cutting off a part of the self. Ironically, Will, who has renounced death, finds death no matter which way he turns. If he chooses Father Weatherbee, he creates the self through a violent rupturing, a form of castration and death; if he chooses Allison, he integrates with his absent center and is reabsorbed into the universe, another form of castration and death. In the end, then, Will's "search" yields no alternative to death.

Notes

[1] Walker Percy, *The Second Coming* (New York: Farrar, Straus and Giroux, 1980) 360.

[2] Lacan distinguishes between the Other (Autre) with a capital 'O' and the other with a small 'o.' The Other which Lacan designates with the upper case 'O' represents language, the site of the signifier, the symbolic order. The Other, then, is the locus of the constitution of the subject. The other which is designated with a lower case 'o' originates with the mother, the first figure in whom the subject identifies itself, as well as the first from which it splits off. For a thorough discussion of Lacanian thought, see Ellie Ragland-Sullivan, *Jacques Lacan and the Philosophy of Psychoanalysis* (Urbana: U of Illinois P, 1985).

[3] Critics have infrequently applied a psychoanalytic approach to Walker Percy's fiction. Three notable exceptions include Susan Derwin, "Orality, Aggression, and Epistemology in Walker Percy's *The Second Coming*," *Arizona Quarterly* 45 (Summer 1989) 63-99, which traces a pattern of ejection and incorporation in the novel; Patrick Samway, S.J., "Another Case of the Purloined Letter (in Walker Percy's *Lancelot*)," *New Orleans Review* 16 (Winter 1989) 37-44, which applies Lacanian theory to *Lancelot*; and Jerome C. Christensen, "Lancelot: Sign for the Times," in *Walker Percy: Art and Ethics*, ed. Jac Tharpe (Jackson: UP of Mississippi, 1980) 107-20; rpt. in *Walker Percy*, ed. Harold Bloom (New York: Chelsea House, 1986) 103-115, which analyzes the relationship between madness and interpretation in Percy's fiction. The paucity of psychoanalytic interpretations is particularly surprising given Percy's knowledge of psychology and psychoanalysis. More specifically, given Percy's medical degree, his publication from 1954 to 1961 of a series of philosophical-psychological essays, one of which was published in the journal, *Psychiatry*, his composition of an unpublished book about the philosophy of language, and his frequently reiterated interest in the study of consciousness (see, for example, his interview with Linda Whitney Hobson in *The Georgia Review* [Spring 1981]), such an approach would seem warranted.

[4] Terry Eagleton, *Literary Theory: An Introduction* (Minneapolis: U of Minnesota P, 1983) 166.

[5] See Ferdinand de Saussure, *Course in General Linguistics*, trans. Wade Baskin (1916; rpt. New York: McGraw-Hill, 1966).

[6] Toril Moi, *Sexual/Textual Politics: Feminist Literary Theory* (London: Methuen, 1985) 99.

[7] Jacques Lacan, *Ecrits*, trans. Alan Sheridan (London: Tavistock, 1977) 709.

[8] Jane Gallop, *The Daughter's Seduction: Feminism and Psychoanalysis* (Ithaca: Cornell UP, 1982) 24.

[9] Gallop 27.

[10] In a non-psychological approach to the novel, Michael Pearson nevertheless observes that Allison clings to the literal and that her name means "the truthful one." See "Language and Love in Walker Percy's *The Second Coming*," *Southern Literary Journal* 20 (Fall 1987) 96. More closely approximating my point, Derwin writes that "in rejecting language she [Allison] has rejected identity as such," 83.

[11] Moi 100.

The Privilege of Maternity: Teaching Language and Love in *The Second Coming*

Shelley M. Jackson

Walker Percy's study of human nature focuses on language and its development. Though he never discusses gender differences in the development of language in his essays, in *The Second Coming*[1] there seems to be an implicit gender difference in language behavior. Unlike Percy's other novels where female characters play subordinate roles to his male protagonists, in *The Second Coming*, Percy has created a female protagonist, Allie Huger, who develops an equivalent relationship with his trademark male protagonist, Will Barrett. Allie becomes the nurturer-healer who first comes to herself, and in turn, helps Will come to himself. In each of Percy's other novels, this role of nurturer-healer has been reserved for men. In this novel, however, Percy utilizes Allie in this role because Will Barrett's search for the lost mother is as vital to him as his attempt to reject the lost father. It also becomes clear that Will must experience maternal qualities usually attributed to women (and embodied in Allie in this novel) before he can come to himself.

As the primary caretaker of the infant, the biological mother, or a substitute maternal figure, becomes the teacher of language. It is not the purpose of this paper to explore the many and varied theories on why women in almost all cultures become the primary caretakers of children, but given that this is the case, it is useful to explore the differences in language behavior that develop in males and females as they interact with the female parent figure. The research of Carol Gilligan in her book, *In a Different Voice: Psychological Theory and Women's Development*,[2] and that of Nancy Chodorow, in *The Reproduction of Mothering: Psychoanalysis and the Sociology of Gender*,[3] shed light on these differences.

Carol Gilligan, a student and later a colleague of Lawrence Kohlberg, maintains that the most widely-acclaimed theories of psychological development, such as that of Kohlberg, have long given short shrift to gender differences. All too often these studies have used male subjects predominantly or exclusively. When female subjects have not fit the patterns that have been established as "normal," the females have been considered "deviant." In reaction to this, researchers such as Gilligan and Chodorow have provided complementary developmental theories which illuminate gender differences. In the interest of maintaining focus and brevity, I have chosen to discuss only the aspects of their research that will be most helpful in providing a reading of *The Second Coming*.

Both researchers agree that gender differences in development occur because one's personality is being formed within a relationship with the mother figure. Chodorow takes an anthropological position: "in any given society, feminine personality comes to define itself in relation and connection to other people more than masculine personality does" because of "the reproduction within each generation of certain general and nearly universal differences that characterize masculine and feminine personality and roles" (43-44). Because the role of woman as caretaker is passed on through the generations, Chodorow maintains that "girls come to experience themselves as less differentiated than boys, as more continuous with and related to the external object-world, and as differently oriented to their inner object-world as well" (167).

Speaking in more psychoanalytic terms, Gilligan draws similar conclusions. She claims that because the mother is the primary caretaker, and because children achieve identity in relation to her, "masculinity is defined through separation while femininity is defined through attachment" (8). In other words, in order for the male child to achieve his masculine identity, he must individuate himself by breaking away from his mother while the female child can individuate while remaining connected to her mother.

Though neither of these researchers focuses centrally on language development, the theories of each can be generalized to the development of language as Dr. Percy perceives it. In *The Message in the Bottle*,[4] one of the ideas that Percy explores throughout the volume is that the process of naming is what spurs language development, and as a result, makes human beings different from other animals. He goes on to write that this process of naming results in intersubjectivity and self-consciousness, two elements of language that indicate its inherent social nature.

Percy describes intersubjectivity as "that meeting of minds by which two selves take each other's meaning with reference to the same object beheld in common" (MB 265). The speaker and the hearer become "co-conceivers and co-celebrants of the object beheld in common" (MB 270-71). It is also important to note that Percy claims intersubjectivity occurs even when one is talking to one's self because speaking requires the positing of a hearer that is distinct from the speaker.

As this intersubjective moment occurs, self-consciousness develops concurrently. Drawing on the work of Charles Sanders Peirce (who Percy claims greatly influenced his ideas on language), David Bleich in *The Double Perspective*[5] calls self-consciousness "the double perspective" or "the double character of one's self" (92). According to Bleich, naming reflects this doubleness because to name is at once to know one's self as distinct from, but also implicated in, others. One comes to know others as one comes to know one's self.

An underlying assumption of these concepts is that language develops within relationship. Herein lies the importance of connecting language development with gender. Chodorow claims that "the most important feature of infantile development is that this development occurs 'in relation to' another person. . . . A description of early development, then, is a description of a social and interpersonal relationship . . ." (77). With Chodorow's idea in mind, it is useful to speculate about what happens when this early relationship between mother and child is less than satisfactory through either the physical or emotional absence of the mother. Percy seems to suggest in *The Second Coming* that the ability to compensate for the language deficiencies suffered through the breakdown of the mother-child relationship is somewhat gender specific.

In Percy's fiction, mother-child relationships are problematic to say the least. Mothers are either conspicuously absent from the lives of Percy's protagonists, or, if they are present, they provide little or none of the nurturing traditionally attributed to maternal figures. Consequently, the emotional and psychological development of these protagonists is hindered seriously. The most dramatic evidence of this hindrance manifests itself in a severe language impediment which makes it difficult or impossible for Percyean protagonists to articulate their feelings clearly and communicate them successfully to others. As a result, they are lonely and isolated.

If these characters are to overcome their isolation, they must overcome their language handicap. In his novels, this requires another maternal figure, as maternal figures are the vehicles of language and consequently of love. Various critics have discussed the absence of the father as that which threatens the demise of Percy's protagonists. Overtly, coming to terms with the absent father is a very real conflict. However, little critical attention has been given to the fact that it is a maternal figure who must help the protagonists relearn language in order to remember, and articulate their pain in order to work through it.

The need for the maternal figure is first suggested in Percy's first novel, *The Moviegoer*.[6] Binx becomes attracted to Kate and tests out his observations about his life and the world with her. Up until this relationship, he has talked seriously with no one, but because Kate "has spells of talking frankly" (M 44), Binx begins to talk frankly as well.

It is not until *The Second Coming*, however, that this maternal figure becomes fully developed. Michael Pearson has called Allie Huger, "the most serious of Percy's speakers to date,"[7] and her importance lies in her ability to help Will Barrett develop self-consciousness and an intersubjective relationship. Through his relationship with Allie, Will can face his father's suicide, and consequently, put his own suicidal notions to rest. Through Allie, Will learns to speak of his pain and to speak of love.

At this point, it is important to note that not all of these "maternal" figures are women in Percy novels. Percival plays this role for the title character in *Lancelot*,[8] and Tom More plays this role for numerous characters in *The Thanatos Syndrome*.[9] I have chosen the term thus far, fully aware of its gender specificity, and consequently, fully aware of its sexist implications. Conceding its problematic nature, I believe it is somewhat appropriate in light of what Gilligan and Chodorow imply about the relationship between motherhood and language. Percy, however, does not speak directly in terms of gender. Maternity as described by Gilligan and Chodorow would, in Percyean terms, best be described as a metaphor, albeit a limited one, for its ability to help create intersubjectivity and self-consciousness in one who does not possess these qualities of language. From this point on in the discussion it will be used with reference to Allie not because of gender, but because she can help Will reconstruct his internal and external object worlds as they are conceived by Gilligan and Chodorow.

In some ways, it is ironic that Allie becomes the nurturer in this novel because of all of Percy's protagonists, Allie is the one on the surface who seems to be the most dysfunctional. She has been diagnosed as so depressed that she has received numerous electroconvulsive shock treatments, and her therapist, in conjunction with her parents, is willing to have her declared legally incompetent. It is also ironic because one of the "symptoms" of the worst stages of her illness—again according to her therapist and her parents—is a severe language deficit. They become most concerned when she stops speaking. She explains that they first have her hospitalized when she forgets the words of a Schubert *lied* during a voice recital at Mary Baldwin.

Given her demonstrated lack of "appropriate" language behavior, one must ask how it can be that Walker Percy creates Allie in the role of nurturer and language facilitator for Will Barrett since her parent figures are as dysfunctional as Will's. It is possible that Dr. Percy is making an observation about gender. Both Allie and Will suffer from deficient parental relationships, but they react to these relationships differently. Will's mother is referred to only once in the entire novel, when D'Lo, the family cook and Will's "mammy," mourns Will's plight after his father's death: "You poor little old boy, you all alone in the world. Your mama dead, your daddy dead, and ain't nobody left in the house but you and me" (SC 275). Will's biological mother is dead by the time Will is twelve, because after his father shoots him, Will recounts his *stepmother's* denial of his father's attempting to kill him. She claimed "that the man had had one of his dizzy spells—he knows with his blood pressure he shouldn't drink and hunt!" (SC 58). (The significance of her reaction will be discussed further on.) The next year, his father is dead, and Will fails to mention his stepmother again.

It would seem that one could look to *The Last Gentleman*[10] for clues to Will's relationship with his mother, but curiously, Will never speaks of her in that novel either except to explain that she was Lucy Hunnicutt whom Kitty's mother knew before they were married. These "absences" bespeak much ambivalence towards his mother on the part of the narrator.

It is apparent from the beginning that Will's parents have failed him miserably. His father is so despairing of the world that he tries to kill Will once his son starts to remind him of himself. Whether he fails on that occasion to commit filicide and suicide intentionally or unintentionally is never clear because after it happens, he claims that both shots were an accident. Will is forty-two years old before he understands the truth. With regard to his childhood, he remembers best his father's despair and the fact that no one in his family ever gave him affection except for a perfunctory hug and kiss at weddings and funerals (SC 57). It is no wonder that Will contemplates suicide repeatedly in the novel until he meets Allie. Using his parents as models, Will had grown up in a home where feelings were denied or had gone unspoken. He has no way of articulating his anger at his parents, or even understanding its existence, so unconsciously he turns it upon himself—until he meets Allie.

Allie's parents, though physically present, are for the most part a destructive force in her life. Allie's mother, Kitty, Will's girlfriend from *The Last Gentleman*, is portrayed in both novels as neurotic and unpredictable. In *Understanding Walker Percy*, Linda Whitney Hobson[11] writes that Kitty "gives no indication that she could carry on an intersubjective relationship with Will" (59). Nor should one assume that Kitty can carry on an intersubjective relationship with anyone else. Allie becomes the victim of her mother's inability to communicate. Throughout the novel, Kitty is unable to understand what her daughter says, responding in the same fashion regardless of whether Allie's responses to her are articulate or not. At one point in the novel, when her mother asks her a question, Allie responds, "Nnnaaaahrgh." In response, Kitty says, "Yes. Well, I agree, honey, it must come as quite a shock" (SC 101). Later, she gets angry at her mother's reactions by telling her to "stop trying to make sense out of my nonsense" (SC 94). Allie's father is even worse. It seems that for the most part, he uses speech to launch verbal assaults. She thinks that he became a dentist so he could attack people with his "mad monologues" (SC 102) while their mouths were full of dental instruments. To Allie, he reacts mostly with silence, and he tries to ignore her and her problems (SC 93).

Though both characters exhibit language deficits as a result of these destructive parental influences, Allie is the only one who sees her problems as reflected in language. Unlike Will, she is conscious of language and its potential, and consequently, she is self-conscious in ways in which Will is not.

As mentioned earlier, one of the events that precipitated Allie's collapse was her failure to sing a *lied* in her voice recital. But close to the end of the novel, she is able to sing it with ease. Will, enamored with her voice upon hearing her sing for the first time, asks her to translate the song, and she explains that it is the song of a lover asking a brook to carry his message of love to his beloved. On more than one occasion, early in the novel, Allie claims that she cannot speak of love because she does not understand what it is. Her inability to sing the *lied* becomes apparent; she could not sing a love song because she did not understand the words. It is only after she comes to know Will and they make love that she can pair word and object, word and action.

While she is in the hospital her psychiatrist, Dr. Duk, tries to give her a "language structure" because he thinks she has none. But Allie is perfectly aware of what he is trying to do, and she explains that she "had stopped talking because there was nothing to say" (SC 87). Dr. Duk's language structures consist of "knock-knock" jokes, not significant verbal exchanges, and Allie realizes their absurdity. In the same conversation, it becomes apparent that her command of language is in some ways more sophisticated than his. Knowing that he knows about stars, she tries to use a star metaphor to explain to him why the shock therapy is not working and why she must be allowed to experience the depth of her depression before she can come out of it. She explains that she must go down to her "white dwarf," (SC 90) in astronomical terms, a star that has collapsed upon itself. Later, when her parents come to visit, she even interprets their conversation for him. When her father says, "Let's get this show on the road, Doc," Dr. Duk looks to Allie to explain what "show" means. Allie explains that her father means, "you and them but not me" (SC 104).

Allie realizes that her parents and her psychiatrist, those who are in charge of her well-being, are far more destructive to her than she is to herself so she escapes the hospital. Percy allows her to assert her self-consciousness immediately. The first word she says aloud after her escape is her name (SC 24). It is also the first word she speaks aloud in the novel. She also reads frequently from her diary which gives her instructions for what to do now that her last shock therapy treatment has temporarily taken away her memory. The destructive influence of her nurturers is never more clear than in this instance. In trying to help her, because of their ignorance, they have attempted to take away her self-consciousness.

As she walks about the town, she begins to try to pair words with objects, but soon realizes that in some cases words have no object with which they are paired, and therefore, they have no meaning for her. She sees a bumper sticker reading "I found it" (SC 24), but she cannot understand its meaning because "it" has no referent. Bemused, she makes her way to her greenhouse to begin her new life.

Allie's sensitivity to language will be exactly that which will allow her to save Will by teaching him intersubjectivity and self-consciousness. They first meet when Will is looking for the golf balls that he has sliced out-of-bounds. As Will lifts the barbed wire fence that marks the boundary of the golf course, the sound of the fence triggers his memory of his hunting trip with his father. As Will contemplates that day, Allie appears, holding his golf balls that have awakened her from a nap by shattering a window in the greenhouse. After she hands him the golf balls, she asks, "Are you still climbing on your anger?" (SC 76). When Will asks, "Angry? No, I'm not angry. Why did you think I was angry?", it is clear that Will lacks self-consciousness in this instance. In his discussion of self-consciousness, Bleich makes a distinction between consciousness and self-consciousness by saying that one can be conscious of sensation, but one is not self-conscious until one is aware not only of the sensation, but of one's self experiencing it. Impatient with her at this point, Will asks her why she was watching him, and she explains that she was not spying on him. She says that she was simply afraid. It becomes clear here who can speak self-consciously. Allie knows what she feels and can communicate it. Will can only begin to explore his anger after Allie has named it for him.

Realizing the impact that talking has on their relationship, after his second visit, Allie "began to think of topics of conversation in case he should come again" (SC 113), only to find that he has not left her, but is sitting on a log near the greenhouse. Will explains that he falls down sometimes, and he needs to rest until the dizziness passes. In her first overt gesture of nurturing, Allie offers to help saying, "That's all right I tend to pick things up. I'm a hoister" (SC 113). Thinking this a flirtation or experiencing embarrassment at her sensitivity, Will says, "We'd make a twosome" (SC 113). But Allie realizes the seriousness of his problem and her solution, and asks him to take himself seriously as well by saying, "Don't joke" (SC 114).

After Will leaves Allie this time, he will not see her again until he falls into the greenhouse from the cave. Allie continues to make improvements in her greenhouse and contemplates how she will integrate herself into the community by finding a job and making relationships with people. With regard to relationships, she decides that she might like to share her life with a man.

Meanwhile, Will continues to do battle with his intrasubjective image of his dead father and with God. Numerous times, he argues with his father while pulling the trigger of the Greener, but there is no intersubjectivity here. His father is dead and cannot hear him. He concludes that the ultimate defeat of his father would be to solve the question of the existence of God, a question Will believes his father never asked. In a bizarre act of bravado, he enters the cave hoping to force God's hand and either defeat both God and his father once and for all, or be defeated by them.

If Gilligan and Chodorow are correct, then the contrast between Will's and Allie's solutions to their problems provides a prime example of the plausibility of gender differences in language development. Gilligan claims that because males must achieve identity through separation, they come to view the world in either/or terms. In other words, males arrive at solutions to problems by putting the proposed solutions in competition with each other and allowing only one to be chosen. Therefore, psychologically speaking, Will must either kill his father or be killed by him. He also must force God to show himself directly or he will die trying. On more than one occasion, he compares himself to Jacob wrestling with the angel: only one can win.

Unlike Will, Allie sees herself not in opposition to the world, but in a position of finding ways to commune with it. Gilligan claims that although males see the world in either/or terms, females look for similarities among seemingly disparate choices and for ways to make connections rather than choose one option to the exclusion of the others. Allie illustrates Gilligan's theory very well. If Chodorow is correct, that females are less differentiated from the external object-world and their inner object-world than males, then females should be able to pair word and object, and create language more easily, even when, like Allie, they have poor parental models.

The premises of these researchers provide a framework for a reading of Part Two of the novel. When Will falls out of the cave, he has not beaten his father or God. Nor will his question be answered in an either/or fashion. Through Allie's nurturing, he will learn intersubjectivity and self-consciousness, and he will learn to orient himself in his world through connection.

Will's rebirth from the womb of the cave, through the bat-infested birth canal into the Edenic setting of Allie's greenhouse, serves its purpose in making Allie Will's new surrogate mother. It is interesting to note that Will's mother was Lucy Hunnicutt, and Allie's full name is Allison Hunnicutt Huger. This seems to be a concrete gesture on Percy's part to recreate his own mother on some level. As Will lies unconscious, she washes him, changes his clothes, feeds him, and tends his wounds until he becomes conscious. While in his drug-induced unconsciousness in the cave, he dreams of a mother gently washing his face. Now his dream has become a reality.

Later, when he falls down on the path as he attempts to get

water, Allie "hoists" him again until they are warming each other, naked under the shelter of blankets and the greenhouse in the midst of a thunderstorm. This time, when she tells him she will pick him up when he falls, there is no more joking on his part. He simply says, "I know" (SC 256). As they begin to make love, Will stops, saying that first he must talk to her. He tells her of his connection to her mother and that her parents want to send her back to the hospital, but then he speaks to her of himself. For the first time, Will can articulate his struggle with his father and with God. And also for the first time, Allie begins to understand love. As Will talks, she wonders, "Was this a way of making love?" (SC 262). On the next page, she concludes, "Even though he was not touching her, his words were a kind of touching" (SC 263). This scene becomes the beginning of intersubjectivity between them that has been made possible by Allie's nurturing.

After this scene, when Will leaves her in an attempt to make plans for their future, he temporarily reverts to his destructive behavior. But this time, Allie's influence allows him to save himself; she has taught him to survive. When he seems at moments to become his former "disconnected" self, thoughts of Allie bring him out of his fugues. While he is drawn to Georgia to the site of the "hunting accident," he sees Allie's hair in the color of the fall leaves and decides to abort the journey. When Will hears his father beckoning him to join him in death, he concludes that his father was in love with death—which was no love at all—and that he wanted life and love with Allie. Her language has become so much a part of him that he begins to think like her, contemplating what Allie would say about his daughter's reaction to his disappearance (SC 290).

When he finally makes his way back to her, Will has made the two most important decisions of his life: he rejects his father's love of death, to choose Allie's nurturing love. He has determined that he will stay with Allie permanently as he explains, "I need you for hoisting and you need me for interpretation" (SC 329). Now Will is using Allie's language, knowing that hoisting means not only picking him up physically when he falls down, but also being his emotional support. And as she lies asleep in his arms at the Holiday Inn, Will listens consciously to his father's voice beckon to him for the final time in the novel. But this time, Will answers with a different voice. Without hesitation, he throws his father's guns over the edge of the cliff and returns to Allie's arms. In one final attack on his unconscious, his father beckons him in a nightmare. But this time, Allie arouses him to consciousness, and they make love for the first time. Afterwards, Will falls asleep and dreams again, and this time he thinks not of the hunting trip in Georgia, but of love. Allie has replaced his father on both a conscious and an unconscious level.

After making love, each can understand love; they can pair word and object, word and act. And for the first time, Will can see the world in terms of connection. Allie has become the mother who can help him connect both his external object-world and his inner object-world. He vows to become a better father to Leslie, and he is capable of it, having internalized a positive parental figure. He decides to build a community for the lonely and isolated so that they will be less so, and he can, because he is less so. And most importantly, there is no longer a question of having God or the world embodied in Allie. He can choose both in connection to each other. Will has found the "it" of Allie's bumper sticker, and this time, the "it" has a referent.

Percy never wrote about gender differences in language. And more often than not, he has been criticized for his fictional treatment of women. But those who see his female characters as facile, poorly developed, and virtually non-existent—to name a few of the criticisms I have read in the scholarship—miss an important point. Many times in his fiction, women, through language in intersubjective relationships, bring his male protagonists to an understanding of their humanity and ultimately save them from self-destruction. It is also possible to conclude that Percy takes things a step further by privileging those qualities traditionally attributed to women without privileging gender. In *The Second Coming,* Allie cannot speak of love until she has experienced it with Will even though she has taught him self-consciousness. In other novels, male characters play this nurturing role. Percival's patience and care allow the eponymous Lancelot finally to ask a question implying the possibility of connection on the very last page. Thomas More, in *The Thanatos Syndrome,* is the nurturing psychiatrist who knows that his clients must talk about their feelings with someone else in order to come to themselves. In *The Second Coming,* Walker Percy agrees with Nancy Chodorow and Carol Gilligan that because of gender identification with the primary language source—the mother-figure—women may find intersubjectivity and self-consciousness easier. But his essays and other novels stress his belief that a person of either gender can, through love and concern, nurture another person into intersubjectivity and self-consciousness and that this crucial "Delta Factor" must be universally acknowledged and practiced. Those who believe that the word, both written and spoken, offers a way out of isolation and that feminist scholarship offers a way of making connections across genders are struggling to articulate what Allie Huger knew all along.

Notes

[1] Walker Percy, *The Second Coming* (New York: Farrar, Straus, and Giroux, 1980).

[2] Carol Gilligan, *In a Different Voice: Psychological Theory and Women's Development* (Cambridge: Harvard UP, 1982).

[3] Nancy Chodorow, *The Reproduction of Mothering: Psychoanalysis and the Sociology of Gender* (Berkeley: UP of California, 1978).

[4] Walker Percy, *The Message In the Bottle* (New York: Farrar, Straus, and Giroux, 1975).

[5] David Bleich, *The Double Perspective* (New York: Oxford UP, 1988).

[6] Walker Percy, *The Moviegoer* (Farrar, Straus, and Giroux, 1960).

[7] Michael Pearson, "Language and Love in Walker Percy's *The Second Coming*," *Southern Literary Journal* 20 (1987): 89-100.

[8] Walker Percy, *Lancelot* (New York: Farrar, Straus, and Giroux, 1977).

[9] Walker Percy, *The Thanatos Syndrome* (New York: Farrar, Strauss, and Giroux, 1987).

[10] Walker Percy, *The Last Gentleman* (New York: Farrar, Strauss, and Giroux, 1966).

[11] Linda Whitney Hobson, *Understanding Walker Percy* (Columbia: UP of South Carolina, 1988).

Rereading Allison Huger: Making Silence Signify in *The Second Coming*

Elinor Ann Walker

While Walker Percy's work is not postmodern in the sense that the work of Pynchon, Barth, or Fowles is, there are gaps in some of his novels that the reader may be required to bridge. Critics have recognized Percy's propensity for ambiguous endings, his philosophical complexity, and the moral questions that his fiction raises. Relative to *The Moviegoer*'s tale of Binx Bolling's search, *The Last Gentleman*'s chronicle of the wandering and wondering Will Barrett, *Lancelot*'s long confession to the silent priest, and *Love in the Ruins*'s examination of the diagnostic tool's potential for both good and evil, *The Second Coming*'s love story appeared to be Percy's most resolved, and most affirmative, statement about the human predicament when it was published in 1980. Although Will Barrett and Allison Huger come upon each other by accident, they seem suited for each other and able to communicate. In Allison Huger, in fact, Percy creates what seems to be a female voice with unexpected authority, and a response to critics who have found his work too idea-heavy, too white, Southern, and male. Some readers, however, might perceive that Allison is still very child-like, as is Will Barrett. If she were a stronger character than Will, she would have no need of him. Her child-like utterances illustrate many of Percy's points about language use and development. Allison Huger's character, then, serves the narrative well in terms of Barrett's quest and Percy's theories. But to read *The Second Coming* not only in the context of Percy's non-fiction, where he articulates his philosophy and the philosophies of Kierkegaard and Marcel, among others, but also in relation to Percy's unpublished notes and drafts for the text reveals two very significant things about Allison Huger. The notes and drafts for this text show that in the unpublished versions, Allison's character is more complex and able to speak more clearly for herself than she is in the published text; the non-fiction clearly supports that she represents a worldview that, in accordance with Percy's own, is redemptive, and even more desirable than her counterpart Will Barrett's.

Unlike Aunt Emily in *The Moviegoer,* whose voice Percy admits is the voice of William Alexander Percy, and other women in Percy's novels, including Kate who can act only when Binx Bolling gives her specific directions in *The Moviegoer,* Kitty the co-ed in *The Last Gentleman,* the adulterous wife in *Lancelot,* the series of women after whom Dr. More chases in *Love in the Ruins,* and even Dr. Lucy Lipscomb who is clearly objectified by More in *The Thanatos Syndrome,* Allison Huger is neither seducer, adulterer, nor, finally, victim. For these reasons, a critic like Michael Pearson may call Allison Huger "the most fully realized of all of Percy's female characters" (90). Pearson also says that "through the fine contortions of Allie's speech and Will's ability to translate . . . Percy makes *The Second Coming* appear to be the philosophical love story toward which the first four novels were building" (91). The love that develops between Allison and Will may be a sign of the grace of God, which Percy seems to indicate both in his notes and in the novel itself, but, ultimately, their falling in love is not the narrative goal. Finally, the reader must push the text several steps further. In Pearson's reading, Allie is subject to Will because he must translate for her; the implication is that her language is meaningless until Will salvages meaning from it. However, the published text shows that Allison creates language and sees signs, and the notes and drafts indicate that Allison is what Will aspires to be. To examine the published version in the context of Percy's notes and drafts also reveals the gap between the two. Allison is significant in the narrative as a representative of Percy's theories and more abstract ideas; she is silenced in the narrative by the boundaries defined by these very abstractions.[1]

Percy's notes indicate that in *The Second Coming* Allison Huger is not only a female extension of Will Barrett, a fictional device that allows him to develop more completely, but that she is also constructed for a specific purpose, to represent a certain philosophical ideology herself. Percy's characterizations of women have not always pleased his critics; often female characters are objects to whom the philosophizing male character reacts. In his notes, Percy indicates that the male character and the female character in the book will speak, think, and act in "two styles" (Walker Percy Papers, Series I, Item E-1aii, 29).[2] Allison and Will use language very differently—Will poses abstract questions, and Allie writes specific notes to herself, tentatively beginning to string words together in sentences. Even though Percy writes in these notes that, as the world defines success and failure, "she [is a] total failure" and he [is a] total success" (Papers, I, E-1aii, 26), finally the notes show, that of the two, Allison is the instrument of grace, the one who signifies a viable approach to life in an imperfect world. She already claims as her own what Will Barrett seeks.

In these rough notes, Percy develops his characters carefully. The male character is a "proud, perfect man" who "wants a sign" of God's existence (Papers, I, E-1aii, 17). It is interesting that, until he gives them the names that appear in the final version, Percy represents the characters using only the signs for a woman and a man (♀ , ♂) (18). This abstract location of their identities makes the overwhelming influence of Percy's theoretical framework (as it is articulated in *The Message in the Bottle, Lost in the Cosmos*, interviews, and other published essays) even easier to identify. Percy's philosophical and semiotic interests inform his preliminary outlines as well as his published fiction. A close examination of the relationship between the characters of Will Barrett and Allison Huger as they appear in the published version of *The Second Coming*, the unpublished notes for the novel, and in relation to parts of Percy's published non-fiction, reveals how inextricably connected Percy's philosophy and fiction are. As this connection becomes clearer, the ideology that Allison Huger represents in turn demonstrates how crucial the character is to the narrative, and how the type of discourse she uses and the changes she effects in language mirror Percy's own philosophy.

Percy characterizes Allison as one who realizes that the problem with language is that most people have forgotten how to use it effectively. People rely on others to define things for them, to tell them not only *what* they are seeing but also *how* to see it. In *The Message in the Bottle*, Percy writes that this willingness to abdicate responsibility characterizes a "consumer." In other words, rather than seeing a thing directly, without mediation, we turn to an "expert," one who knows. In this role, we reduce an object to a specimen. Percy cites the example of the Grand Canyon; guidebooks and authorities prepare the spectator for a certain view, and the sightseer values his or her encounter with the place only in so far as it conforms to what it "should" look like, thereby losing the wonder and the delight of the discovery. Of such a person, Percy writes, "the source of his delight is the sanction of those who know" (*The*

Message in the Bottle 55), and his plight Percy terms the "loss of sovereignty." This abdication robs the individual of seeing the place, the idea, the work of art without mediation. One gets only a partial glimpse, then, and experiences the world vicariously, seeing not as one ordained with a gift of vision, but as a consumer in need of a translation, a prescribed view.

To exist in this state is to be passive, even blind, for in the ability to see and to articulate what one has seen, every person is sovereign and possesses a gift that sets him or her apart from other living creatures. In "Naming and Being," Percy writes,

> No matter whether I give a name to, or hear the name of, a strange bird; no matter whether I write or read a line of great poetry, form or understand a scientific hypothesis, I thereby exist authentically as a namer or a hearer, as an I or a Thou—and in either case as a co-celebrant of what is (*Personalist* XLI [1906]: 153-54).

There is a relationship, then, between naming and hearing, writing and reading, forming or understanding, existing as an I or a Thou. Human beings use language primarily to communicate with one another, and to communicate well one must be able to listen as well as talk. This communion bridges the gap between one person and another and may dispel loneliness, or even despair.

Percy's novels often trace his protagonists' development as "sovereign wayfarers" (*Message* 60). To act as a "sovereign way-farer" is to be "a wanderer in the neighborhood of being who stumbles into a garden" (60). What is inherent in the recovery of sovereignty is the recovery of language. In accepting the position of wayfarer, a person acknowledges that he or she is not at home in the world, that the moments of belonging achieved through communication happen in a state akin to grace. To Percy, "the old words of grace are worn smooth as poker chips and a certain devaluation has occurred, like a poker chip after it has been cashed in" (116). This devaluation necessitates a new way of speaking in order to make the smooth pieces rough and distinctive once more. When language, whether or not it is religious, lends vitality to an object, person, or place, it achieves a renewal.

To describe something in an unfamiliar or indirect way, using metaphor, for example, to couple two things that are not usually paired, pulls meaning out of its void and puts it back into language. Metaphor "seems to be all wrong: it asserts an identity between two different things. And it is wrongest when it is most beautiful" (*Message* 67). Percy finds truth in things that seem "all wrong." His characters often follow this pattern; they are confused, and time is out of kilter. They suffer from amnesia, deafness, alcoholism, or fugue-like states, and bump around in the present, colliding occasionally with something or someone long enough to regain a sense of place. This disorientation serves a purpose, though, precisely because these characters view the world differently. Percy's characters take the reader by surprise, so that he or she too must step back from what is considered normal and witness the world as the protagonist sees it, suffering the same disorientation.

In the characters of Will Barrett and Allison Huger in *The Second Coming*, Percy creates two figures whose peculiarities recreate a fictional world. Both Allie and Will Barrett literally "stumble into a garden," which is an old greenhouse on some property that has been left to Allie. She seeks its refuge after she has escaped from a mental institution where she has undergone shock treatments. Disillusioned with the modern world and suffering from falling spells, Will Barrett retreats to a cave to escape the "great suck of self" (*The Second Coming* 14). Will enters the greenhouse inadvertently when he falls into it after his self-imposed exile to Lost Cove Cave, where he had retreated to wait for God to give him a sign, once and for all, of His existence. The very name of the cave—Lost Cove—evokes the novel's more obvious themes: the "loss of love" (death, betrayal), the "cost of love" (crucifixion, salvation).

In *The Last Gentleman*, in which Will Barrett first appears as protagonist, he is the classic consumer; someone else must tell him if he has witnessed a sign. Indeed, he wants Sutter Vaught to do all of his seeing for him. At the pivotal baptism scene, he asks Sutter, "What happened back there?" (*Gentleman* 317). Will cannot see the sign for himself; he wants Sutter to define salvation. Sutter will not answer the engineer's questions; he tells Will, "I can't help you. Fornicate if you want to and enjoy yourself but don't come looking for me for a merit badge certifying you as a Christian or a gentleman or whatever it is you cleave by" (179). In *The Second Coming*, Will poses the most abstract question: does God exist? What he discovers is that theorizing about such notions as grace and salvation (and the signs thereof) does not provide many answers.

No longer questioning those who are not qualified to give him the news of his salvation, Barrett decides that he will go straight to the source, so to speak, and give God the chance to make an announcement of his existence. He rejects the prescribed view of God, Jack Curl's testimony of religion. Barrett asks Curl, the chaplain, if he believes that God exists, to which the chaplain answers affirmatively. Will proceeds to tell Curl his plan: "the question can be put in such a way that an answer is required. It will be stipulated, moreover, that a non-answer, silence, will be construed to mean no" (*Coming* 139). Curl responds, "'There you go' . . . It made him uneasy to talk about religion" (138). The "expert" here is uneasy in his own field. Rather than pushing Curl on the subject, Barrett creates his own strategy to get his question answered. But he does not die a slow death in the cave; he contracts a toothache and falls from his perch on a ledge, becomes half-crazed with pain, abandons, in a sense, his original intent, and seeks a way out of the cave, ultimately tumbling into Allie's greenhouse. His salvation, then, may or may not be an act of God; Percy does not say that God afflicts Will with the toothache. The description of Will's fall into the greenhouse does seem to be a figurative return to the garden, where he is tended by Allie and nurtured back to health. He plummets "through air and color, brilliant greens and violet and vermilion and a blue unlike any sky, a free-fall headfirst with time enough to wonder if he might not be dead after all" (226). This fortunate fall provides Barrett with the time and freedom to communicate with another human being, despite their respective oddities, so that the novel's conclusion conveys a sense of closure and fulfillment.

Like Percy, Will Barrett constantly questions the mysteries of existence and tests theory after theory, but he becomes more and more prone to complicated abstract thoughts that may in some way be symbolized by his falling spells. Allison Huger, on the other hand, dwells only in the present moment. While hospitalized for schizophrenia, she receives shock treatments which effect short-term memory loss. When Allie's doctor tries to convince her to have one final shock treatment, she argues, "I have to go down first. You're trying to keep me up" (*Coming* 90). She has worked out an elaborate astronomical metaphor for her psychic state: "A red giant collapses into a white dwarf. Hard and bright as a diamond. That's what I was trying to do when my mother found me in the closet going down to my white dwarf" (90).[3] Allie is trying to discover a self that is "hard and bright." She formulates her own language, her own pattern of speech. Again, Percy's early drafts contribute more details. In the unpublished notes, she is waiting and watching for a sign:

> After twelve hours, maybe more, in the closet, she began to see a star. It did not surprise her. Some sign, she knew, would be given her if she waited long enough. Even as she became weaker, hungrier, the conviction

> grew in her that she would not die if she waited. That was not the way things worked. True, things did not make much sense. But if you waited them out, a kind of sense could be wrung from them. One came into a dark place and waited. After a while she saw the star. Then the star came closer and entered her. She became the star. (Papers, I, E-2ai, 13).[4]

Allison internalizes the sign here with no mediation from doctor or parent. Like a child, she does dangerous things with language and strings together words that have never before existed together in the same sentence, determined to wring sense from these sounds. Her affliction lends a certain creativity to her thoughts, and she illustrates what Percy calls "metaphor as mistake." The scene in Percy's notes obviously parallels Will's experience in the cave. But while Will seeks to escape his solipsism, Allison needs to realize the potential of selfhood. She wants to recreate herself, give birth to something, rewrite her life's script.

Like Will, Allison has a plan; she decides to escape from the mental institution, but in order to insure that she will know what to do, she writes her instructions to herself. This self-directing is the first step that Allie takes toward redefining who she is. She begins to see herself not as her doctor and her family do, but as a person who has a right to feel the way that she feels: "To tell you the truth, I'm not even sure that I am sick. But they think I'm worse because I refuse to talk in group (because there is nothing to say) and won't eat with the others, preferring to sit under the table (because a circle of knees is more interesting than a circle of faces)" (27). Her logic makes sense; she is silent because she has nothing to say. Because she uses "more interesting" instead of "less intimidating" to describe the knees under the table, her observation is funny, not pathetic. Allie takes words very seriously, "to mean more or less what they said, but other people seemed to use words as signals in another code they had agreed upon" (34). Because of her short-term memory loss, Allie is able to pierce through to the heart of a word, to its original meaning, before overuse and misuse robbed it of its significance. Allie articulates what Walker Percy means when he discusses the "devaluation" of language: "Words surely have meanings, she thought, and there is my trouble. Something happens to words coming to me from other people. Something happens to my words. They do not seem worth uttering. People don't mean what they say. Words often mean their opposite. If a person says to you: *I hate to tell you this, but*—she doesn't hate to tell you. She likes to tell you. This is a good place to make a new start with words" (82).

In this sense, then, Allie is a sign-maker. Will is a sign-seeker.

In his notes Percy writes, again using the symbols for male and female, that the woman is "out of it—getting in" and the man is "in it—getting out" (Papers, I, E-2aii, 1). The woman exists in time that is "fractured," the man in "linear" time (2). When they meet, what Percy terms "zone crossing" (2) occurs. In "Symbol as Hermeneutic in Existentialism," Percy writes, "In the situation-in-which-we-find-ourselves, two zones can be delineated, the zone of the nought and the zone of the other" (*Message* 284). Percy interprets Sartre and Marcel here, explaining that when human beings name something, they not only validate its existence, but they also make that object "a static and isolated entity" (283). The irony is, of course, that while human beings can name other objects, there is no simple way to know and identify the self. For this reason, Percy believes that people fall into a sort of frenzy of possession; if they can acquire material objects which they can easily call by name—a car, for example—then perhaps the owning of that object will "inform" (284) one's own identity. The problem is that this "consumption of goods" (284) always fails. Rather than "informing" the person, a material possession just becomes sucked into a person's inability to name him or herself, the void around the person, into the "zone of the nought" (284), the "sovereignty of having and the exclusion of the other's having" (284). The "zone of the nought" is the realm of the self, and there is only one way to counter the emptiness—isolation, despair—that threatens to consume the self. Allison has been stripped of her possessions, forced to become like other patients, and Will is struggling to shed his past existence. Allison is trying to get down to her real self; Will is trying to escape the "suck of self" (*Coming* 14). Will waits in the cave, surrendering his destiny to God, if God exists. Allie escapes the institution in order to take control of her life. Will calls into question the content of the world; Allie calls into question the content of the word. Both characters illustrate how word and world are connected when Percy allows their zones to cross.

What each character must discover is how to bridge the space between two individuals using language that, in the past, has only broadened that distance because of its "devaluation" (*Message* 116). Allie's own speech follows peculiar patterns because of her schizophrenia, but what is surprising is that her mistaken utterances often reveal that her perception is sharper than that of so-called normal people. Her particular, and as society defines it, peculiar viewpoint allows Allie to penetrate the barriers that keep people from understanding each other. Percy's preliminary drafting of the novel reinforces that Allison is able to see clearly and to describe what she sees in new ways. One particular scene in *The Second Coming* focuses on Allison's thoughts as she glimpses some women in a car. The women seem very removed from her in the published version—they are not described in detail but are dismissed as "leafers," or those who have come to see the autumn spectacle, and they are from Florida (86). In Percy's unpublished drafts of the novel, however, Allison sees that the women are "motionless as dolls. Yet surely, she thought, they were talking and laughing. Yes, if one looked closely, it was possible to see their lips move" (Papers, I, E-2ai, 1). Allison is the feminist reader here. She recognizes and articulates that these women speak and act behind a barrier, just as she does. The closer look reveals that these glassed-in faces speak; Allison can only guess at what they are saying. "[The car's] occupants, the four women, seemed to be seated in a row. Their lips moved. What were they saying? She imagined that one, the driver, said, *no, this is not the place*" (Papers 13). This succinct utterance of alienation and Allison's reading of it indicates that, as Percy developed Allison's character, he allowed her to identify with these muted women and to decipher their language. Ironically, as a fictional character who is a spokesperson for Percy's philosophy, Allison also remains behind the glass, the boundary established by her creator, the author, who chose not to include this scene in the novel's final version. The passage in the unpublished version figuratively articulates the difficulty of being heard and of finding some ground from which to speak. Allison is the "sovereign wayfarer," the "wanderer in the neighborhood of being who stumbles into a garden" (*Message* 60), the one who recovers language. Percy's early drafts seem to enhance his characterization of Allie, and the unpublished notes define her as one with sharp, original vision.

Allison refines her vision when her dependence on her family and her willingness to be defined by their standards collapses; she learns to reject the opinion of the "experts." Percy calls Allie "cunning" in his notes for the novel (Papers, I, E-2aii, 8). Allie carries out her plan to escape with cunning and stealth and plots her course meticulously, down to the very time of day (although she is unsure of the year). She openly defies her family by leaving her therapy, and arms herself with a "knapsack . . . the smallest sleeping bag she could find . . . a Boy Scout knife, a Scripto pencil, a pocket notebook, a comb, a can of neat's foot oil, a box of candles, and a small bag of food" (*Coming* 23). She is preparing herself for the dive into the wreck, as it were. With these essentials, she succeeds not only in writing her own life but also in taking care of herself. Allie proves that she is capable of existing without the mediation of an institution and its therapists; she no longer needs shock treatments to jar her into reality.

For example, as Allie is making her home in the greenhouse, she decides to move an old stove inside the greenhouse; the stove has a compartment for wood and will provide warmth as well as a means of cooking. The difficulty is that the stove is tremendously large and heavy, but Allie figures out that with a block and tackle arrangement she will be able to move it. Barrett offers to get some men to help her, but she rejects his offer of help, explaining, "Because there I will be with people having put the stove where I want it. And that's the old home fix-up which is being in a fix. Then what? The helping is not helping me" (112). The "old home fix-up" is interference, mediation, a step removed from doing the thing by herself. Allie resolves the fundamental need for warmth by herself, and she asserts the desire to do so. She lets Barrett know that the men in her life, namely her father and her doctor, have maintained a certain amount of control over her. Now she wants to know how Barrett fits into the plan. Allie demonstrates courage in her adherence to the decision that she alone has made; she will move her source of heat unassisted.

However, she does accept a verbal suggestion from Will. He defines a "creeper" for her as the "platform on wheels which mechanics lie on when they work under cars" (114) and suggests that this means of transportation would enable her to move the stove after she tugs it out of the ground. As he leaves, Allie thanks him "for the word" (115). The exchange indicates that these two are learning how to communicate. Together, they create and share a vocabulary. Will observes and respects Allie's boundaries, she is willing to accept a word from him but not his physical strength. Allie asserts her ability to function independently of Barrett, but she does not refuse to communicate with him. The stove, then, becomes her treasure, "a castle of a stove, a rambling palace of a stove, a cathedral of a stove, with spires and turrets and battlements" (203). Because Allie is solely responsible for its disinterment, she is able to rename the stove so that it becomes a "castle," a "palace," a "cathedral." The ensuing description of the stove makes it a thing of beauty:

> Panels of porcelain enamel, turquoise blue for the oven doors and the four warming closets, little balconies jutting out head-high, snowy white for the splashback,

> were fused to heavy cast iron between frames of nickel. Bolted on one side was a nickel-iron box lined with heavy copper and fitted with a spigot. A water reservoir! On the other side, the firebox with a bay window of a door glazed with panes of mica, some crazed, some crystallized, but all intact (204).

In effect, in the Walker Percy scheme of things, Allie rescues the stove from its ordinariness and redefines it so that once again it has significance. The irony is, of course, that few women would be inclined to attach salvation to a stove. In fact, the stove still limits Allison to a domestic sphere while Will Barrett is dodging bullets and hunting golfballs. But that Allie has unearthed the stove and successfully exposed it to air is clearly significant in the narrative. Once again, Percy indicates that Allie has given birth, but instead of reaching some inner star, she has exhumed a stove. Perhaps the irony is unintended. Percy has Allison name herself a "hoister" (113) and thus indicate her strength.

Attempting to reach her true self, Allison focuses on the immediate, the concrete, while Will is busy trying to find some sort of system or ideology by which to live, to escape the confines of self. Like Will, Allison may use figurative language, but her descriptions tend to focus on specific details. Her description of the stove, for example, is very concrete. Will, on the other hand, is likely to make sweeping statements that are filled with explosions of color, "brilliant greens and violet and vermilion and a blue unlike any sky" (226), or to ask grand rhetorical questions: "[w]as it love or failure of love?" (148). His father's system has not worked; Jack Curl's system does not work. Yet Will persists in his abstract endeavor. Ironically, he desires concrete proof for what cannot be proven; God finally does not give him proof of his existence. Because of the tangible pain of a toothache, Will lands in the greenhouse, Allie's concrete world. The encounter and subsequent relationship with Allison prompts him to question, "[i]s she a gift and therefore a sign of the giver?" (360). Finally, he accepts Allison as a "sign of the giver." Even in Will Barrett's world, Allison remains a sign of something larger, and not significant in and of herself.[5] Will reads Allison in the same way that the unpublished text invites us to read her; as representative of an ideology, a system of belief, a theory of language, and renewal. Not a bad role to play in a text, to be sure. But what does Will Barrett signify for Allison?

The Second Coming, Percy's notes and drafts for the book, and his published non-fiction where he more fully explains his ideas all establish Allison's importance to the narrative. While Percy afflicts her with too many physical and psychological problems (amnesia, anorexia, and schizophrenia) in the notes and drafts, these early versions contribute to Allison's development as a character. Being a creator and namer gives her a great deal of power in Percy's philosophical system. The published text shows that Allison realizes the potential for misreading when she makes "two discoveries. One was that you didn't have to talk in complete sentences. People didn't seem to need more than a word or two to make their own sense of what you said. The other discovery was that she could talk as long as she asked questions. Making a statement was risky—" (*Coming* 4-5). This risk derives from miscommunication, the failure of one person to read another person carefully, to listen and decipher each signal, every word, before superimposing an interpretation that may or may not be correct. In *The Second Coming*, the character of Allison Huger is not only a spokesperson for Percy's language theories, but she is also a female character who writes her own directions, creates her own language, and speaks and interprets carefully. Percy has also said the "novelist is a namer" (Personal Interview, 2-8-87). This connection legitimizes Allison as an authoritative female voice in Percy's fiction, but without the gloss of the earlier notes and drafts, it is too easy to read *The Second Coming* as a continuation of Will Barrett's story and to read Allison as the prize Barrett receives at novel's end. Percy, who was after all a father and a doctor, a diagnostician of modern day malaise, and a theorist prone to abstractions himself, also maintains control over Allison Huger the character. The reader, however, may study Allison as carefully as she studies the women in the car, waiting and watching for the next word.

Notes

[1] Although all of Percy's characters, whether male or female, are defined to some degree by the philosophical ideologies underlying their development, Allison's character is constructed so that, in the published text, she is more a representation of a language theory than a representation of a person.

[2] Percy's manuscripts—notes, drafts, and revisions—are housed in the Southern Historical Collection, Round Wilson Library, University of North Carolina, Chapel Hill. All subsequent references will be noted simply—Papers, Series, Item, and page number. Permission to quote from the Papers in this essay has been graciously granted by Mrs. Walker Percy.

[3] In the notes for the novel, Allison is medically diagnosed as an anorexic who is trying to become small enough to locate the essence of her identity.

[4] Earlier in this section, Percy writes, "In the dark closet where she had been found curled up and rigid she thought she saw a star. The star had come from her. That is, she had given birth to it" (I, E, 2ai, 4)

[5] The reader who is familiar with Percy's concept of news and newsbearer may see Allison as a sort of newsbearer whose outlook is relevant to Will Barrett precisely because he is, in Percy's terms, a "castaway" desperate for an answer to his predicament. Allison's love may be a sign of the grace and love of God. Nonetheless, it is not Allison who would be ultimately responsible for Barrett's ability to take something—God's existence, for example—on faith. Percy writes in his essay "The Message in the Bottle" (again referring to Kierkegaard) that faith is "a setting aside of reason," "not a form of knowledge" (*Message* 145). Will turns to Allison just as he has turned to his father, to Sutter Vaught, to Jack Curl. He wants someone else to show him the truth, to tell him how to live.

Works Cited

Pearson, Michael. "Language and Love in Walker Percy's *The Second Coming.*" *Southern Literary Journal* 20.1 (Fall 1987): 89-100.

Percy, Walker. *The Last Gentleman.* 1982. New York: Farrar, Straus, and Giroux, 1977.

—. *The Message in the Bottle. How Queer Man Is, How Queer Language Is, and What One Has to Do with the Other.* 1984. New York: Farrar, Straus, and Giroux, 1954.

—. "Naming and Being." *Personalist* XLI (1960): 153-54.

—. Personal Interview with Elinor Ann Walker. 8 February 1987.

—. *The Second Coming.* New York, Farrar, Straus, and Giroux, 1980.

—. Walker Percy Papers in the Southern Historical Collection, University of North Carolina, Round Wilson Library, Chapel Hill.

A Gentleness with Women: Loving, Caring, and Sexual Dilemmas in Walker Percy's Fiction

Anneke Leenhouts

In the confrontation between Binx Bolling and his great-aunt near the end of *The Moviegoer* she tells him:

> More than anything I wanted to pass on to you the one heritage of the men of our family, a certain quality of spirit, a gaiety, a sense of duty, a nobility worn lightly, a sweetness, a gentleness with women—the only good things the South ever had and the only things that really matter in life. (M 224)

Of the aspects of Walker Percy's fiction that deal with the end of Southern tradition and its aftermath the one examined least concerns relations with women. Although Percy's male protagonists are occupied with women a good deal in thought as well as in deed, curiously little attention has been paid to the nature of these imagined and actual relationships in the light of the old values' demise. Yet the incapacity of Percy's male character to achieve a balanced relationship, i.e. a relationship based on social, intellectual, and sexual equality, is in many ways the clearest manifestation of the failure to reconcile traditional views with the post-traditional world.

Walker Percy has made it clear that much in his first two novels had to do with William Alexander Percy: "The whole thing is a dialectic between his attitude, which *was* a Southern paternalism, and the attitude of the two young men . . . a more detached, alienated point of view."[1] It is worth noting in this context how in Will Percy's life as set down in *Lanterns on the Levee* the mother figure is hardly present. In *The Moviegoer*, Binx Bolling has been brought up in his great-aunt's house; of his mother he says that "Sometimes I have the feeling . . . that who my mother was depended on the chance selection of a supervisor of nurses in Biloxi" (M 48). In *The Last Gentleman*, it is the father's family traditions and principles which come to the fore. Binx claims he can barely remember his father, and his contacts with his mother and the children of her second marriage have been counterbalanced to some extent by his aunt's teachings. Accordingly, he is far removed from great loves and great obsessions. He has opted for an ordinary life, selling stocks and bonds, an apartment in nondescript Gentilly. He has affairs with his secretaries, though, this being New Orleans in the late 1950s, he does his own hiring and marriage is not on the agenda. "It is," he declares, "not a bad thing to settle for the Little Way, not the big search for the big happiness but the sad little happiness of drinks and kisses, a good little car and a warm deep thigh" (M 135-36).

Percy contrasts Binx's attempts to seduce his new secretary, Sharon Kincaid, with his relations with his aunt's step-daughter Kate Cutrer. In the end it is Kate, not Sharon, he becomes involved with sexually, and at her instigation rather than his own. When called to task by Aunt Emily, he has no defense to offer: "'Were you intimate with Kate?' . . . 'I suppose so. Though intimate is not quite the word'" (M 222). It is left to Kate to reconcile their actions—Binx's agreeing to take her along on a business trip to Chicago because she is low and possibly suicidal and utterly incapable of coping with the social obligations of Mardi Gras—with the proper romantic excuse, the announcement that they are to be married. Binx takes Kate on without any illusions about her true state. His persistent honesty, for that matter, is what decides Kate: "I don't know whether I love you, but I believe in you and I will do what you tell me" (M 197). By the end of *The Moviegoer* most of Binx's choices in life have been made: he has married Kate, returned to the Garden District, started medical school. He is, in short, in the first stages of living " . . . a long useful life serving my fellowman." Little is said of Kate beyond the observation that she has "fattened up" and continues to see her analyst.

In *The Last Gentleman*, after five years of psychiatric treatment that have taken every cent of his inheritance, Will Barrett is still incapable of coming to terms with his father's suicide and the concept of honor that provoked it. Although the house he has inherited was full of women—his step-mother and numerous aunts—even before his father's death, they appear not to have influenced Will's life in any noticeable way. Only the black cook, D'lo, is presented as a source of surrogate motherly love. Will falls in love with Kitty Vaught, it soon becomes clear, because she is as uncertain of her role as he is of his. An Alabama girl who has spent most of her young life studying ballet, she has reached the stage where turning twenty-one without ever having had a boyfriend becomes a problem in urgent need of remedy. She is attracted to Will because he is safe. As her brother Sutter's ex-wife Rita sums it up: "You're the girl who can't talk. And he can't remember. That makes you a pair" (LG 63).

On the subject of women Will has been told by his father: "Go to whores if you have to, but always remember the difference. Don't treat a lady like a whore or a whore like a lady. . . . If you do one, then you're going to be a fornicator and not caring. If you do the other, you'll be . . . fornicator and hypocrite" (LG 100-01). It is, as has been pointed out by Broughton, the "whole question of human sexuality and morality . . . distilled . . . into a matter of social distinction."[2] No moral objections are raised against the taking of sexual pleasure as such outside the confines of "honorable" love and marriage, providing the proprieties are adhered to. In fact, we later learn that Will's father, Ed Barrett, was taken at age sixteen to a whorehouse in Memphis by his father in order not to have him "worrying about certain things," a course of action not repeated in Will's day, though clearly not because of any moral scruples on his father's part.

Will desires above all that love should run its proper course:

> It was part of his expectations of the life which lay before him that girls would be girls just as camellias were camellias. If he loved a girl and walked with her on Folly Beach by moonlight, kissed her sweet lips and held her charms in his arms, it should follow that he would be simply he and she she . . . (LG 167)

Thus Kitty's experiment "by Kitty for the benefit of Kitty" in Central Park goes so drastically wrong: "proper" love cannot encompass the "lady" assuming the "whore's" part by taking the sexual initiative. Will's courtship of Kitty Vaught steers an uneven course between the dictums of Ed Barrett and Kitty's own sorority girl inclinations on the one hand and the influence exerted by Rita Vaught on the other.

Rita, New Mexico social worker and New York businesswoman, widely-travelled, cultured, is Percy's first portrayal of an independently successful woman—indeed, it comes as something of a surprise to learn that Rita is from Georgia. Rita has taken the impressionable Kitty under her wing, but while Kitty looks on Rita as a combination elder sister/surrogate mother, Rita's motives are described with far greater ambivalence. Rita believes, Kitty tells Will, "that anything two people do together is beautiful if the people themselves are beautiful and reverent and unselfconscious in what they do" (LG 179), but on at least one occasion Sutter Vaught suggests that Rita's interest in Kitty stems from lesbian tendencies on her part. Despite Rita's apparent encouragement of his suit, Will himself wishes away any sign of exotic dress or outspoken speech attributable to Rita's influence. Kitty "was his sweetheart and ought to know better." Will loves Kitty when she behaves according to established patterns; the moment she develops her own initiatives, especially in the romantic field, he is at a loss.

Why Will does not marry Kitty, accept her hundred-thousand-dollar dowry and the job offered by her father is never made clear, but when she reappears in *The Second Coming*, it is a very different, self-assured Kitty unabashedly out to grab what she can get. She and her husband resort to bribery in an attempt to have their daughter Allie declared legally incompetent, so that they can divide her inheritance between them. Moreover, she repeatedly stresses her own availability to Will, leaving him as confused by her initiatives as ever: "Did Kitty want what she appeared to want? Did she want him to fuck her in the summerhouse? Yes! . . . A violent shiver took hold of him. . . . What was he afraid of? . . . that he shouldn't? that he couldn't?" (SC 712). Will's mixed reactions show that he still has not achieved what he wanted so urgently in *The Last Gentleman*, for once and all to "get the straight of this lady and whore business." He has sidestepped the issue very neatly in his own marriage to Marion Peabody, Northern, very rich, crippled by polio, not pretty but very much in love with him and married for all of those reasons, rather than any great passion on his part. His recollections of their married life focus on the dutiful, caring aspects of his role as a husband: the central image is Will pushing Marion's wheelchair.

Will's dealings with Allie Huger are made to appear honorable primarily by default. Confinement to a mental institution and subjection to electroconvulsive therapy have left her with her wits intact but otherwise at a loss and incapable of dealing with the everyday world. She is not so much a more vulnerable version of Kitty at twenty-one as another Kate Cutrer going down into herself and not possessed of relatives with enough money and sense of obligation to rule out commitment—in Allie's case to a clearly second-rate institution at that. Will proposes marriage, legal steps to safeguard Allie's considerable property, and love in the late afternoon to keep the demons at bay. For his part, he will renounce the Peabody inheritance, go back to work, build a house, help to raise a family. In short, it is Will's objective to start afresh with, at last, someone who will be "simply she."

Stock romantic images appear and reappear in Percy's novels to varying effect. Will's mother, Lucy Hunicutt, romantically recollected by Mrs. Vaught from a dance at the old Tate Springs Hotel long ago, becomes Lucy Cobb from Georgia dancing to the "Limelight" theme with Lancelot Lamar, both of them "in love" and hence in need of few words. Allie thinks of love with Will Barrett as "a dancing in the Carolina moonlight with the old world and time before you" (SC 255). Will and Kitty, when they attempt to dance, make an ungraceful pair, primarily because Kitty is not light on her feet for all her ballet training. Will's "pinning" of Kitty to signal an informal sort of engagement becomes Sarge, the jewelry salesman, pinning Allie with four different sorority pins during their week of sexual experimentation in Nassau, or Raine Robinette wearing Lance's daughter Lucy's sorority ring. The dream of innocent, pure love similarly descends from Kitty's actual confused "changeling" state to Allie, "buzzed" and feeling "like a rape victim in every way but one" to, ultimately, Lance Lamar's assertion that the girl Anna in the room next to his, a victim of horrifying multiple rape, is the new Virgin: "Her ordeal has made her like a ten-year-old" (L 159).

Lancelot is Percy's most extensive as well as most extreme discourse on the aspects of love. Lancelot Lamar kills his second wife, Margot Reilly, for her adultery, which has resulted in his acknowledging a daughter he did not father and which she makes increasingly less effort to hide as the story progresses. In contrast to the decorous Lucy Cobb, Margot imbues Lance's love for her with physical obsession. She sleeps with him on their first meeting, reversing their roles both in this initiative and in bartering for marriage: her body and her millions in return for Lance's old name and the chance to restore his decaying mansion. Having achieved her objective on both counts, socially accepted and with nothing left to restore, she becomes bored and looks for new adventures. On the eve of her death she informs Lance that she is leaving him to play Nora in a new film version of *A Doll's House*. If Margot, daughter of a self-made millionaire from Odessa, Texas, seems relatively straightforward in her wants and needs, loving in equal measure "a good piece in Henry Clay's bed and Henry Clay's bed itself," Lance is doomed to frown on the very assertiveness that holds him in thrall physically. Margot's money and drive cause him to neglect his law practice and turn to drink, in other words, to become as ineffective a man as his father was, a third-rate poet who took money from the Huey Long administration he professed to despise and turned a blind eye to his "delicate" wife's affair with a travelling salesman. Hence Lance's turning to the memory of his great-grandfather, the man who fought a savage duel with Bowie knives over the imputation that his mother had had sexual relations with a black man. Thus, for Lance, "a gentleness toward women" becomes inextricably bound up with "a stern code . . . an intolerance of swinishness . . . and above all a readiness to act, and act alone if necessary . . ." (L 157). By her actions Margot has forfeited her entitlement to gentleness—the reader has been forewarned by being told on a number of occasions that her actions are like a man's. In the confrontation between ethereal Lucy Cobb, dead of leukemia, and flesh-and-blood Margot, it is the traditional image that wins out. Given that, as Bertram Wyatt-Brown specified in *Southern Honor*, "a male's moral bearing resided not in him alone, but also in his women's standing,"[3] the insult to Lance's masculinity and his name cannot be allowed to pass. Margot's lover Jacoby is killed with the great-grandfather's Bowie knife; Margot herself dies in the explosion that wrecks Belle Isle.

Lance Lamar's story is told in retrospect from the institution where he has been confined. At the end of the novel he is discharged, "psychiatrically fit and legally innocent." Like his ancestor before him, he has escaped punishment for killing in defense of his good name. We are told that he does not mind that Belle Isle was destroyed; rather, he plans a future in simpler, less ornate surroundings approaching those of his ancestors' pioneering days and with an equivalent moral order:

> There will be leaders and there will be followers. . . . There will be men who are strong and pure of heart. . . . There will be virtuous women who are proud of their virtue and there will be women of the street who are there to be fucked and everyone will know which is which. You can't tell a whore from a lady now, but you will then. (L 178)

He plans to marry Anna. "I shall love and protect her. I can make her well" (L 159). He is astonished when Anna refuses to accept his view of her as a person to be remade after the loss of herself in the degradation of rape. Her retort, "Are you suggesting . . . that I . . . my person can be violated by a *man*? . . . Don't you know that there are more important things in this world?" (L 251) echoes Margot's earlier dismissive "Sex. You men set so much store by it. . . . Believe it or not, I've found something more important than the almighty penis" (L 174).

Lancelot equates the assertion of sexual independence with the denial of virtue. Binx Bolling and Will Barrett are less extreme, but they also turn to women made vulnerable by mental and physical debilities. Even Thomas More, the least ancestrally preoccupied of Percy's narrators, professes relief at having escaped marriage to his cousin Lucy, doctor, planter, intensely capable woman: "An unrelieved disaster it would have been . . ." (TS 348). Binx Bolling, Will Barrett, Lancelot Lamar, and Thomas More are each descended from old, honorable landed families, sons of doctors and lawyers and themselves professional men or in the process of becoming so. They are no longer tied to the land—Binx Bolling sells his duck club, Will Barrett has put his plantation in the soil bank. Belle Isle is opened up to tourists for the money, then done up in excess of its former glory and subsequently destroyed. Thomas More eventually makes his home in a luxuriously equipped former slave cabin. All of Percy's protagonists have been required to come to terms with a world in which the traditions of their forefathers no longer apply and with the cost of tradition's demise to their own father. Yet for all their adjustment to the present-day world they by and large retain their ancestor's outlook on women. Though they love, love is subordinate to caring for and taking care of. Relationships are founded in inequality—social, intellectual, and, since the women are expected to be proper, sexual inequality. It is not so much a case of new customs doing away with old traditions as of the old paternalistic attitude of male-female domination adapting to modern times.

Notes

[1] Barbara King, "Walker Percy Prevails," *Southern Voices* 1 (May-June 1974): 20.

[2] Panthea Reid Broughton, "Gentlemen and Fornicators: *The Last Gentleman* and a Bisected Reality" in Broughton, ed., *The Art of Walker Percy: Strategems for Being* (Baton Rouge: Louisiana State UP, 1979) 102.

[3] Bertram Wyatt-Brown, *Southern Honor: Ethics and Behaviour in the Old South* (1982, rpt. New York: Oxford UP, 1983) 53.

From Silence and Madness to the Exchange That Multiplies: Walker Percy and the Woman Question

Elzbieta H. Oleksy

One of the commonest criticisms of existentialism has been its narrow focus on individualism and subjectivity. Most existentialists posit the ideal of a kind of superman who is inevitably always male. One can hardly imagine woman as a subject in existentialism. Would Kierkegaard, for instance, conceive of woman as a Knight of Faith? Had he read Hawthorne, he surely would have been surprised to see how many characteristics of the true Knight of Faith, that solitary quester embarked on what he calls "existential pathos," lingered in the portrayal of Hawthorne's woman with the letter.

In his imaginary interview with Camus, Robert C. Salomon asks the writer-philosopher the question that, I believe, was never posed in Camus's lifetime:

> RCS: I must ask, for you speak continually of "man"—man's fate, man's happiness, man's responsibility—what about *women*? What, if I may ask, about *Missus* Sisyphus?
> CAMUS: [a quick smile, then very serious] Well, in French as in English, the word "man" is a general term including both men and women.
> RCS: Yes, but you seem to evade the point. All your characters, for example, are men. Your women are silent.
> CAMUS: As my mother was silent, but no less significant for that . . .

This essay was previously published in *The Southern Quarterly* 31 (Spring 1993) 58-68, and is reprinted here by the generous permission of Stephen Flinn Young, editor, *SQ*.

> RCS: But the mother in *The Stranger* is dead when the novel begins. Meursault's girlfriend Marie is little but a pretty face, a warm body; we know her only by her smell, her giggle, her laugh.
> CAMUS: Meursault isn't much more.
> RCS: Yes, but Meursault is at least a character; Marie isn't even a foil.
> CAMUS: That's true, but the mother's presence is what defines the novel.
> RCS: It's true, that's so, but the point is, again, she isn't a *character*. And *The Plague*: it's all men. *The Fall*, a man; *The Myth of Sisyphus*, all about the absurd *man*, the absurd hero, Don Juan, Kafka, all men, often womanizing men.
> CAMUS: I'm guilty, I suppose. There is Martha in my plan *Malentendu*, but yes, you're right, and I admit, I distrust women. I am thoroughly dependent on them, but they do not share my world.
> RCS: Would you say that existentialism is primarily a male philosophy?
> CAMUS: That isn't my concern. But you might ask Simone. (80-81)

And Simone de Beauvoir, prompted by the sexist existentialism of her contemporary compatriots, argued for the concept of the *other*, which sees woman not as an end in herself but as an auxiliary in man's important quests.

Recent feminist criticism takes pains to identify Simone de Beauvoir as the foremother of feminism, but not without reservations. According to Janet Todd, de Beauvoir's *The Second Sex* is not very useful for feminist theory on account of its tendency to "universalize as nature rather than historicize as culture the distinctions of men and women" (18). De Beauvoir is trapped, Todd contends, in a "rationality defined by and for men," whereby *consciousness* is conceived as *maleness*. De Beauvoir, Todd aptly concludes, cannot "appropriate for feminism the Sartrean notion of free *subjectivity* and self-defining agency without becoming 'contaminated' by the profoundly sexist ideology of objectivity to which this notion is inevitably coupled." Existentialism philosophically sanctioned phallocentrism. By conceiving subjectivity as essentially male, existentialism relegated woman to the position of the other. As Toril Moi has written, "patriarchal [existentialist, in Moi's terms] ideology presents woman as immanence, man as transcendence" (92). Though we usually associate such views with twentieth-century European existentialism (specifically, Sartre and Camus), which in turn was indebted to American modernism, we might benefit from looking at what Søren Kierkegaard has to say on the subject of woman's immanence:

> When woman is determined as virginity, she is thereby characterized as being for an other. Virginity is, namely, a form of being which, insofar as it is a being for itself, is really an abstraction and only reveals itself to another. The same characterization also lies in the concept of female innocence. It is therefore possible to say that woman in this condition is invisible. . . . Logically, this contradiction will be found to be *quite in order*, and he who knows how to think logically will not be *disturbed* by it, but *will be glad in it*. (74, emphasis added)

Walker Percy's indebtedness to existentialism (and specifically to Kierkegaard) has been pointed out so often that there is no need to belabor it here. Suffice it to say that from *The Moviegoer* through *Lancelot*, Percy defines consciousness as exclusively male. As long as Percy remained under this influence, he was virtually unable to create meaningful relationships between men and women. Not only is his portrayal of womanhood distorted in the novels prior to *The Second Coming*, but also his male characters' inability to forge and develop meaningful relationships results from these distortions. It was only after Percy moved away from this sphere of influence that his fiction boasted a rounded depiction of womanhood and a fully meaningful relationship.

Throughout his fiction, Percy connects the rejection and victimization of women with men's fear of their sexuality. In *The Moviegoer*, Binx shies from Kate's "not whorish bold but theorish bold carrying on" (200) to the point of impotence. Will Barrett in *The Last Gentleman* can "hardly" consummate his union with Kitty. In *Lancelot*, Lance Lamar disintegrates under the sexual demands of his second wife, Margot. And the later Will, fresh from discovering the joy of love and sex combined, repeats his old cliche, musing about Kitty's "special boldness" and concluding that "women grow more lustful as they grow older" (322).

In Percy's fiction, sexual women are "punished" in a number of ways for the sexuality that misogyny has conventionally stigmatized. Kate loses all "self" by becoming willessly integrated into the paradigm of male authority: she has to be told what to do and say to the point where her individuality becomes totally erased. She says to Binx: "If I marry you, will you tell me: Kate, this morning do such and such, and if we have to go to a party, will you tell me: Kate, stand right there and have three drinks and talk to so and so?" (197). In *Lancelot* the metaphor of silence and self-annihilation becomes literalized when Margot and Raine are murdered by Lance, thereby *losing* themselves in all senses. Even mothers, female children and good wives (that is, those who are neither "theorish" nor "whorish" bold) are depicted in stereotyped misogynistic images; Lance uses the sexist attributes of "scissoring legs" and "boring fists" for his mother, his first wife Lucy and his daughter Siobhan alike.

By any feminist standards, this would suffice to ban Percy's works from the feminist syllabus on the grounds of sexism. Or, on the contrary, one might join the scholarly chorus of those who still think that gender issues are not of vital importance to Percy's worldview. Adopting either of the two attitudes, however, means confusing the identities of author and character in Percy's fiction. Percy's male protagonists (the epithet sounds tautological, for prior to *The Second Coming, all* Percy's protagonists were male) fail, if not in their quests, then surely in their relationships with women. And their failure in forging and developing relationships with women stems not only from their incomprehension of women in their lives, but also from the nature of their goal: a unique (read: performed solitarily) quest for faith the realization of which could be threatened by a relationship with a "separate" female individual. Binx exemplifies what Northrop Frye calls a "stylized figure" (306), a carrier of Kierkegaard's notion of the Knight of Faith. The younger Will wavers among several contending forces in a fashion reminiscent of Jake Horner in John Barth's early novel, *The End of the Road*, sooner resembling an allegorical agent than flesh and blood man. And Lance, likewise embarked on a quest of sorts, epitomizes the characteristics of Percy's earlier protagonists in his incapacity to understand, let along love, *any woman*.

Nonetheless, it would be a gross exaggeration to say that the extreme case of Lance or Percy's other male protagonists voice their author's convictions about women. If such were the case, why did Percy make of Lance such a pitiful, if not revolting, figure? Why, in the final episode of *The Moviegoer* do we come to pity not only Kate, whom Binx "hands along" her journey downtown, but also Binx himself? If Binx's role in their marriage amounts to just this "handing along," then he surely picked up the right profession (at the conclusion of the novel he enters medical school). And why, in *The Last Gentleman*, did Percy make Will miss the import of the crucial scene of Jamie's baptism, just the way Kate missed a parallel event in *The Moviegoer*? Why, in other words, does the Percy protagonist almost invariably fail? Percy provides the answer to these questions in an interview with Bradley R. Dewey on the subject of his debt to Kierkegaard's thought, where he confesses his unease with

Kierkegaard's notion of subjectivity. What he finds lacking in subjectivity is, in Percy's words, an "understanding or an explanation of intersubjectivity—caring for the other person" (*Conversations* 119).

Critics have traditionally looked for intersubjective bonds in almost every novel Percy wrote. Linda Whitney Hobson perceives such a union in several odd couples: Binx and Kate, Binx and Lonnie, Will and Sutter, Lance and Percival, Tom and Ellen.

If Percy indeed approached intersubjectivity in each of his novels, he never fully explored it before *The Second Coming*. In *The Message in the Bottle*, Percy defines intersubjectivity as "that meeting of minds by which two selves take each other's meaning with reference to the same object held in common" (265). In each of these novels the subjectivity explored is invariably that of one person, and invariably male. In three of the five "couples" Hobson lists, the second "self" (Lonnie, Sutter and Percival) is entirely, or almost entirely, absent from the narrative as the subject. The unique character of intersubjectivity is transpersonal togetherness, reciprocity, if you will. We cannot really judge if the intersubjective communion has taken place if we do not witness it in the "presence," in Gabriel Marcel's understanding of the word, of the other. It is not until *The Second Coming* that two consciousnesses, female and male, meet in intersubjective communion. And it is Will Barrett, in *The Second Coming*, who ultimately understands, if not women, then a woman.

In his interview with Jan Nordby Gretlund, Percy said that after he finished *The Second Coming*, he felt "as if [he] had been a woman who had been pregnant four years." He compared his condition to a postpartum depression. "I went into a terrible depression," he said, "and all I knew was that I would never write another novel as long as I lived" (*Conversations* 215). Not only does Percy, like Pushkin having written *Eugene Onegin*, significantly identify here with feminine experience, but also the latter part of the quotation underlies the point I wish to argue—namely, that *The Second Coming* terminates a period in Percy's literary career.

Whether or not Percy intended it, the gang-raped mute Anna (also, the mute girl in *The Last Gentleman*, with whom Will Barrett recalls playing Chinese checkers in the hospital where he was treated for amnesia) and Allison Huger in *The Second Coming*, who loses her language and then reinvents it, bring to mind what recent feminist criticism has to say on the subject of the repression of femininity. According to Mary Jacobus, femininity is "the repressed term by which discourse is made possible. The feminine takes its place with the absence, silence, or incoherence that discourse represses" (29).

Of course, it is always possible to trace the motif of a mute girl in his fiction to Percy's traumatic discovery that his first daughter was born deaf and mute. A look at what transpires in recent southern women's writing, however, bluntly reveals how very symptomatic of the transformation of southern womanhood Percy's mute and insane females are. One might resort for additional insight to the classic Derridean ambivalence as regards woman's writing: both to remain silent and to speak (write) is to conform to the structure of the phallocentric logos, one through repression, the other through contradiction. Hence, to write, for a woman, means either to stay sane accepting, or conforming to, the phallocentric logos (as some southern women authors, for instance, Anne Tyler and Shirley Ann Grau, indeed do), or to work "ceaselessly and simultaneously," says Elizabeth Meese, to deconstruct it. The nonconforming violators of the logos, Meese argues, are "mad [angry] about the specific oppressions that have written women's historic condition" (120). Though the complexities of recent southern writing created by women need not be rehearsed here in detail, Meese's argument appears to be extremely pertinent to the works of such authors as Jill McCorkle, Ellen Gilchrist, Gail Godwin and Lisa Alther.[1] To remain sane and at the same time defy the logos is to subvert it through language as, for instance, Alice Walker does in *The Color Purple* (a book Percy greatly admired). In *Lancelot*, when Anna recovers her language it is precisely to defy Lance and through defiance to challenge the language and culture of patriarchy.

Interestingly, the creation of Anna in *Lancelot* resembles Hélène Cixous's metaphor for a woman's life. Cixous says: "She [a sleeping beauty] sleeps, she is *intact*, eternal, absolutely powerless. He has no doubt that she has been waiting for him forever: ("Sorties" 66, emphasis added). Lance dreams not of a relationship with Anna, but of her virginity and her domestication. He tells Percival that the violation Anna suffered (she was gang-raped) has in a sense "restored her virginity, much as a person recovering from the plague is immune to the plague" (86). He relates to Percival his dream of domestication in which Anna played the "New Woman":

> There was perfect quiet. Yet I was not alone in the house. There was someone else in the next room. A woman. There was the unmistakable sense of her presence. How did I know it was a woman? I cannot tell you except that I knew. Perhaps it was the way she

> moved around the room. Do you know the way a woman moves around a room whether she is cleaning it or just passing time? It is different from the way a man moves. She is at home in a room. The room is an extension of her. (36)

However, says Cixous, "once awake (him or her [even this ambivalence is very much present in Lance's narrative, for Anna's silence parallels Cixous's 'sleep,' whereas Lance narrates his own dream]), it would be an entirely different story. Then there would be two people, perhaps. You never know with women. And the voluptuous simplicity of preliminaries would no longer take place" (66). And Anna "awakens" when Lance propounds his theory of *felix culpa* and defies Lance in these words:

> "Are you suggesting," she said to me, "that I, myself, me, my person, can be violated by a *man*? You goddamn men. Don't you know that there are more important things in this world? Next you'll be telling me that despite myself I liked it." (251)

It is, however, Allison Huger in *The Second Coming* who effectively subverts phallocentrism with her unique argot and her consciousness. She is one of the most seductive female characters in contemporary American male discourse. Percy surely intended Will, and not Allison, to be the protagonist of *The Second Coming*. But Allie somehow got out of hand and took over the narrative.

Allison is a recent escapee from a psychiatric institution where she was treated for schizophrenia. It rather goes without saying that her failure at living is as obvious a story of privation as that of Esther Greenwood of Sylvia Plath's *The Bell Jar*. Before she gathers strength and courage to flee from the asylum, the phallocentric logos is defined for her by her father, her first lover and the Pakistani doctor who tends to her in the asylum. The names of the latter two ("Sarge" and "Dukipoor," the latter of which, as John Hardy interestingly notes, means "legion" [190]) and the mannerisms of her father (reminiscent of General Patton, Allie reports—an echo of Plath's "panzer man") evoke military associations. Moreover, Allison, reminiscing about the moments of intimacy with Sarge, thinks that pleasing him was like "doing well" for her father ("look at my report card, Daddy, straight A's. A Plus in music"). She asks herself: "But what do you do after you get straight A's for Daddy and Sarge?" (109). The answer, for Allison, was to seek compensation and forgetfulness in drugs and, after her mother discovered her lying in the closet "with the shakes," in silence.

Allison, who after her flight from the asylum, is reborn into the world like Rip Van Winkle (her own analogy) or like Chief

Bromden on a fishing trip, finds her voice to utter her name aloud:

> At first it sounded strange again but strange in a different way, the way an ordinary word repeated aloud sounds strange. Her voice sounded rusty and unused. She wasn't sure she could talk. (27)

Percy, echoing Freud's question "What do women want?" in two interviews, one before, one after the publication of *The Second Coming*, ostensibly seems to be much more aware of the feminist issue than he wishes to acknowledge. The saga of Allison's survival in the greenhouse meticulously records her tasks, which require tremendous physical strength and competence and which she accepts with surprising matter-of-factness. In Percy's words, "she was a hoister, a mistress of mechanical advantage. And here was something to hoist. If she could hoist this monster of a Grand Crown stove, she could do anything in life" (230). Her real problem is with words and, specifically, with naming. She says that "naming is knowing" (107) and in these words she expresses one of the most central feminist concerns. As Dorothy Smith puts it, "We are confronted virtually with the problem of reinventing the world of knowledge, of symbols and images" (16).

Allison speaks with disarming directness. At times, her words are full of wisdom. At other times, and especially when she confesses her emotional turmoil, her language verges on adolescent ingenuousness. Whereas Will's chapters are marked by (characteristic to the Percy hero) irony, often verging on cynicism, Allison's passages are permeated by an intelligence whose strength and warmth color the entire narrative and are unchecked or unguarded by irony.

As Allison and Will's relationship develops, they both agree that it will be founded on a unique difference. They both concede that Will needs Allison for "hoisting" (he tends to fall), and she wants him to "interpret" her language to others (one really wonders why; her idiom seems to be as effective as any one can find). Even if these reciprocal tasks might suggest androgyny, in the sense that the masculine here implies logic and the feminine "masculine" physical strength, they in fact triumphantly transcend androgyny, since the female and male selves are more than opposite; they are complementary gender identities which must be united to make true selfhood possible for each.[2] They are intimately combined selves, sharing the same human consciousness, and their relationship is defined more by similarities than by differences. As Allison tells Will, "[W]hy is it that I seem to have known you before I knew you. We are different but also the same" (298).

The book not only presents the second coming of Will Barrett, Kitty Vaught and Sutter (in *The Second Coming* a hearsay figure), but it also "reincarnates" Anna from *Lancelot* as Allison Huger. Percy has Kitty, Allie's mother, interpret what an old black cook has once said of Allie, "That chile don't belong in this world," as an acknowledgement of Allie's incomplete reincarnation. Kitty says that "Allie had come from another life but had not quite made it all the way" (325), which may indicate that Allie belongs to both narratives, *Lancelot* and *The Second Coming*, which in turn implies her second coming as a fictional character, though it can also carry a number of meanings, several of which are suggested by Kitty.

Towards the end of the book Kitty tells Will that prior to Allie's confinement in the asylum, she discovered her daughter lying in the closet with the "shakes," obsessively repeating, "I'm no good, I'm a liar, I'm the original hooker" (327). Kitty apparently consulted a certain Ray ("a true mystic") and learned that Allie's previous incarnation was "a courtesan spy for the North in Richmond." "Don't you see?" Kitty tells Will. "Then she was too much of this world, she knew too many men, talked too much, lied too much, and abused her body. So now she is not of this world, knows nobody, can't talk enough to lie, doesn't use her body at all" (327). The whole passage is playfully tricky and suggests a number of possibilities. Most obviously, a "hooker" is a prostitute. But the word "hooker," which derives from a "hook," in nautical slang signifies an "anchor," whereas the verb may signify "to pull," for instance in golf jargon. Admittedly, in reference to Will, Allie fulfills the functions suggested by both meanings. When Will complains to Allie of his black-outs, she tells him that she can "hoist" him. But we may derive even further meanings working on the assumption that, as Percy says in his essay on Melville, the "freedom and happiness of the artist is attested by his playfulness, his tricks, his malice, his underhandedness, his naughtiness, his hoodwinking the reader. So happy is the metaphorical distance between the novelist and his narrative that he's free to cover his tracks at will" (42).

Percy's hoax reminds one of John Fowles's in *A Maggot*, where a fictitious courtesan, Rebecca Lee, is an eighteenth-century Joan of Arc and Mother Lee, the founder of the Shakers. Her intelligent individual Dissent overcomes the forces of the past and paves the way for the women's liberation movement. The clues Percy supplies in the book point to his playful handling of the Shakers' dogma and ritual, yet the conclusion we can reach upon closely scrutinizing these clues is most crucial for our understanding of the book's theological issue.

It might be interesting to note that recent concern in redefining women's history has generated new interest in Shakerism by feminist theologians. Though they are far from reaching a consensus on whether or not Shakerism is feminist (one of the main obstacles seems to be the Shakers' traditional division of labor), they still seem to concede that the most revolutionary element of Shakerism was the elevation of woman to an equal spiritual position with man.

Allison, we recall, was, prior to her confinement in the asylum, discovered lying in the closet with the "shakes." Her confinement and the story of her mistreatment in the hospital bring to mind Mother Ann's imprisonment in a "house of correction," which period, in particular, marked her ascendancy as the leader of the sect. The Shakers fully credited the story of her martyrdom in prison, where she claimed to have been treated with utmost cruelty. Edward Deming Andrews debunks this myth, pointing to various inconsistencies in Ann Lee's account, but perceives its significance in exemplifying "the persecutory complex" commonly demonstrated by the early adherents of the sect (5). Likewise, Allie evokes through memory her treatment in the hospital, which constituted primarily of ECT, which she calls "buzzing" or "frying." She says, "Fried is crucified" (119), which qualifies Allie for a literary incarnation of Christ or, rather, the second embodiment of Christ in the figure of Mother Ann.

The sect's separation from the world is realized in Allison's flight from the asylum and in her solitary dwelling in the greenhouse. Her particular idiom harbors the notion of "speaking-in-tongues." Fowles pertinently refers to the words of Ann Lee as "Logos," for the historical Ann Lee proclaimed upon receiving her calling, "I am Ann the Word." Needless to say, the theological importance of this statement intersects with the focal feminist concern. Allison's instinctual and competent handling of Will after his experiment in the cave parallels the Shakers' ability to heal the sick. In one of the sources as regards Shakerism we learn of their "hugging lift" (Lamson 81). No doubt, Allison's last name suggests Percy's playful adaptation of this source. Even the division of the narrative into Allison's and Will's alternate chapters evokes the sect's insistence that "the sexes be separated and organized along independent yet parallel lines." The Shakers' ideology of equality and partnership between men and women is realized in Allison and Will's relationship. The scene, which embraces the idea of partnership, prepared for by Will and Allison's assertion of their reciprocative tasks, constitutes one of Percy's masterstrokes:

> They stayed in bed all day and all night except for meals, loving and laughing, frolicking, exchanging many a kiss and smacks on the ass while carts creaked outside and maids tapped on doors with keys. Frowning, she peered closely at his cheek and squeezed a blackhead. He straddled her thighs and rubbed her back, sore from hoisting, pressed his thumbs in the two dips at the bottom of her spine, marveling at how she was made. Each tended to the other, kneading and poking sore places. She examined him like a mother examining a child, close, stretching skin, her mouth open, grabbing hair to pull his head over to see his neck, her eyes slightly abulge with concentration, checking his cave wounds, picking at scabs. When her eyes happened to meet his, they softened and went deep. (390-91)

Not only does the Percy hero for the first time give of himself to a woman, but also the ritual of caretaking clearly expressed here remakes the rigidly fixed gender roles. The scene expresses sensuality and a caretaking which heals or, in Cixous's words, "a love that rejoices in the exchange that multiplies" ("The Laugh" 887).

Will and Allie respond to each other's loneliness, but their relationship will not be exactly a *solitude à deux*. With the money he has inherited, Will wants to found a community on a piece of property Allison has inherited. It will consist of two crippled builders, a gardener, and an assortment of social outcasts. They will inhabit Allison's greenhouse, and they will grow fruits and vegetables. This pastoral retreat, once again reminiscent of Shakerism, coupled with the promise of love and marriage, constitutes, no doubt, Percy's alternative to stagnant existence (what he calls "the living death") and social corruption. And the book's final paragraph makes it quite clear, even as it alludes to the idea of male and female messiahship inherent in the Shakers' doctrine, that Will not only has his existence provided for but, in addition, has the existence of God proved to him, once and for all, by the act of giving:

> Will Barrett thought about Allie in her greenhouse, her wide gray eyes, her lean muscled boy's arms, her strong quick hands. His heart leapt with a secret joy. What is it I want from her . . . he wondered, not only want but must have? Is she a gift and therefore a sign of a giver? Could it be that the Lord is here, masquerading behind this simply silly holy face? Am I crazy to want both, her and Him? No, not want, must have. And will have. (411)

Notes

[1] See Donna Kellerher Darden, "Southern Women Writing about Southern Women: Jill McCorkle, Lisa Alther, Gail Godwin, Ellen Gilchrist, and Lee Smith," *Southern Women*, ed. Caroline Matheny Dillman (New York and London: Hemisphere P, 1988) 215-220.

[2] For the discussion of androgyny in *Lancelot*, see my article "Walker Percy's Demonic Vision," *Walker Percy: Novelist and Philosopher*, ed. Jan Nordby Gretlund (Jackson: UP of Mississippi, 1991) 201-02.

Works Cited

Andrews, Edward Deming. *The People Called Shakers*. New York: Dover, 1963.

Cixous, Hélène. "The Laugh of the Medusa." *Signs: Journal of Women in Culture and Society* 1.4 (1976): 875-94.

—. "Sorties: Out and Out: Attacks/Ways Out/Forays." *The Newly Born Woman*. Trans. Betsy Wing. Minneapolis: U of Minneapolis P, 1986. 63-132.

Frye, Northrop. *Anatomy of Criticism*. Princeton: Princeton UP, 1957.

Hardy, John Edward. *The Fiction of Walker Percy*. Urbana and Chicago: U of Illinois P, 1987.

Hobson, Linda Whitney. *Understanding Walker Percy*. Columbia: U of South Carolina P, 1988.

Jacobus, Mary. *Reading Woman: Essays in Feminist Criticism*. New York: Columbia UP, 1986.

Kierkegaard, Søren. *A Kierkegaard Anthology*. Ed. Robert Bretall. New York: Modern Library, 1938.

Lamson, David R. *Two Years' Experience Among the Shakers . . . 1948*. Rpt. New York: AMS Press, 1971.

Marcel, Gabriel. *The Existential Background of Human Dignity*. Cambridge: Harvard UP, 1963.

Meese, Elizabeth. *Crossing the Double-Cross: The Practice of Feminist Criticism*. Chapel Hill: U of North Carolina P, 1986.

Moi, Toril. *Sexual/Textual Politics: Feminist Literary Theory*. New York: Methuen, 1985.

Percy, Walker. *Conversations With Walker Percy*. Eds. Lewis A. Lawson and Victor A. Kramer. Jackson: UP of Mississippi, 1985.

—. "Herman Melville." *New Criterion* 213 (Nov. 1983): 42.

—. *Lancelot*. New York: Farrar, 1977.

—. *The Last Gentleman*. New York: Farrar, 1966.

—. *The Message in the Bottle*. New York: Farrar, 1975.

—. *The Moviegoer*. New York: Knopf, 1961.

—. *The Second Coming*. New York Pocket Books, 1981.

Salomon, Robert C. *Introducing the Existentialists: Imaginary Interviews with Sartre, Heidegger and Camus*. Indianapolis: Hackett, 1981.

Smith, Dorothy E. "Ideological Structure and How Women Are Excluded." *Canadian Review of Sociology and Anthropology* 12.4 (1975).

Todd, Janet. *Feminist Literary History*. New York: Routledge, 1988.

Contributors

Lewis A. Lawson teaches at the University of Maryland, College Park. He is the author of *Following Percy* and co-editor, with Victor A. Kramer, of *Conversations with Walker Percy* and *More Conversations with Walker Percy.*

Emory Elliott teaches at the University of California, Riverside. He is the editor or author of *Power and the Pulpit in Puritan New England, American Colonial Writers, 1735-1781, Puritan Influences in American Literature, Revolutionary Writers: Literature and Authority, American Writers of the Early Republic, Columbia Literary History of the United States,* and *Columbia History of the American Novel.*

Timothy K. Nixon is a graduate student at the College of William and Mary.

Susan V. Donaldson teaches at the College of William and Mary. She has written articles chiefly on southern writers. Currently she is working on a book on Eudora Welty and a study of writers and painters in the modern South.

Doreen Fowler teaches at the University of Mississippi. One of the principal organizers of the annual Faulkner and Yoknapatawpha conference in Oxford, she co-edited the conference volumes from 1979 to 1989. She is the author of *Faulkner's Changing Vision: From Outrage to Affirmation* and articles on American and English literature in such journals as *American Literature, The Journal of Modern Literature,* and *Studies in American Fiction.* She is presently working on a psychoanalytic reading of Faulkner's novels entitled *Faulkner: The Return of the Repressed.*

Shelley M. Jackson is currently completing her dissertation on contemporary southern women writers at the University of Maryland. In 1993 she directed a program of interviews with such contemporary southern writers as Pat Conroy and Hodding Carter for the Smithsonian Institution. Her article on Josephine Humphreys appeared in the *Mississippi Quarterly*.

Elinor Ann Walker recently completed her Ph.D. in English at the University of North Carolina, Chapel Hill. She has contributed articles on Elinor Wylie, Carolyn Kizer, and Mona Van Duyn to *The Oxford Companion to Women's Writing in the United States* and published articles on Jill McCorkle, Josephine Humphreys, and Jorie Graham.

Anneke Leenhouts received her Ph.D. from Rijksuniversiteit Utrecht. She has studied at Duke and the University of Virginia on a Harkness fellowship. She is a translator in the Netherlands.

Elzbieta H. Oleksy is the director of both the North American Studies Center and the Women's Studies Center, University of Lodz, Poland. She has taught at the University of Pittsburgh, SUNY at Buffalo, and Southern Seminary College. She was a recipient of a Fulbright grant in 1977-78, and American Council of Learned Societies fellowship in 1983, and the Kosciuszko Foundation scholarship in 1990. She is the author of numerous articles in American and European journals and of *Battle and Quest: The American Fable of the Nineteen Sixties*. Her study of Hawthorne and Percy, *Plight in Common*, appeared in 1993.

Index